# Nature and Young Children

## Second edition

Now in its second edition, *Nature and Young Children* promotes the holistic development of children by connecting them with nature. It offers advice and guidance on how to set up indoor and outdoor nature playspaces as well as encouraging environmentally responsible attitudes, values and behaviour in your early childhood setting.

Covering topics as diverse as gardening with young children, creating an accessible nature program for children with special needs and addressing cultural differences in connecting children with nature, this book reveals how important nature play can be in the development of young children.

This user-friendly book offers guidance on

- alternative settings for nature-focused programs;
- international approaches to nature play in early childhood;
- the role of the adult in outdoor learning;
- using nature play for cross-curricular learning;
- integrating nature education and peace education;
- health and safety.

This highly accessible book will provide all early years practitioners, teachers and students of early childhood courses with a wealth of ideas on how to foster creative play and learning in nature-focused environments while also promoting positive connections with nature.

**Ruth Wilson** has over 30 years' teaching experience as a teacher and teacher educator. Most of her work over the past 20 years has focused on connecting children with nature.

# Nature and Young Children

Encouraging creative play and learning in natural environments

Second edition

**Ruth Wilson**

Routledge
Taylor & Francis Group

LONDON AND NEW YORK

Second edition published 2012
by Routledge
2 Park Square, Milton Park, Abingdon, Oxon OX14 4RN

Simultaneously published in the USA and Canada
by Routledge
711 Third Avenue, New York, NY 10017

*Routledge is an imprint of the Taylor & Francis Group, an informa business*

© 2012 Ruth Wilson

First edition published by Routledge 2008

*British Library Cataloguing in Publication Data*
A catalogue record for this book is available from the British Library

*Library of Congress Cataloging in Publication Data*
Wilson, Ruth A., 1943–
Nature and young children : encouraging creative play and learning
in natural environments / by Ruth Wilson. – 2nd ed.
    p. cm.
Includes bibliographical references and index.
ISBN 978-0-415-52673-9 (hardback) – ISBN 978-0-415-
52674-6 (pbk.) – ISBN 978-0-203-11935-8 (ebook)
1. Science–Study and teaching (Early childhood)–Activity
programs. 2. Early childhood education–Activity programs.
3. Nature study. 4. Natural history–Outdoor books. I. Title.
LB1139.5.S35W55 2013
372.35′7–dc23                                            2012002380

ISBN: 978-0-415-52673-9 (hbk)
ISBN: 978-0-415-52674-6 (pbk)
ISBN: 978-0-203-11935-8 (ebk)

Typeset in Bembo
by HWA Text and Data Management, London

MIX
Paper from
responsible sources
FSC
www.fsc.org    FSC® C004839

Printed and bound in Great Britain by the MPG Books Group

For children and the Earth –
and all the wonderful people who shared ideas and
information about special places for young children

# Contents

# Illustrations

## Photographs

## Tables

## Boxes

# Abbreviations

| | |
|------|------|
| C&NN | Children and Nature Network |
| ECEE | Early Childhood Environmental Education |
| EE | Environmental Education |
| EEI | Education and Environment Initiative |
| EIC | Environment as Integrating Context |
| NAAEE | North American Association for Environmental Education |
| NACC | Nature Action Collaborative for Children |
| NAEE | National Association for Environmental Education |
| NAEYC | National Association for the Education of Young Children |
| RSPB | Royal Society for the Protection of Birds |
| SANC | Schlitz Audubon Nature Center |

# Introduction

Those who contemplate the beauty of the earth find reserves of strength that will endure as long as life lasts.

(Rachel Carson)

Play – it's natural for young children. We see children engaging in play almost from the moment of birth. They play with their hands; they play with sounds; and they play with almost anything anywhere.

Animals and adult humans engage in play, as well. Play has the unique quality of adding joy to our lives. At times, we engage in play simply to express delight and joy. We do it for fun! For many animals, play allows youngsters to practice hunting and other survival skills. For them, play serves a critical role in developing mastery in such skills as running, balancing, and reading the environment for signs of danger and sources of food.

Children play because that is what they are naturally inclined to do, but play for them is a lot more than filling time. Play helps prepare children for what they may do and experience later in life – for example, what roles they might assume as adults in a family and community (parent, teacher, dancer, firefighter, etc.); how creative they will be in solving problems and expressing ideas; and how well they relate to others and the places where they live. Play during childhood is, in fact, required for children to reach their full potential (Stephens 2009).

For children, play serves a multitude of developmental functions – physically, socially, cognitively, and emotionally. Play provides motivation and practice in each of these areas. When given the opportunity to play freely, children will test their limits physically – how high they can climb; how much weight they can lift; how far they can throw; how fast they can run. They'll also be testing their courage and building their self-esteem. Socially, they'll practice cooperation and sharing, leading and negotiating, making friends and standing up for one's self. Cognitively, play helps children develop in the areas of creativity, logic, and problem-solving. It helps them explore, experiment, and discover. Play also contributes to children's emotional development. As they experience joy, togetherness, and accomplishments, they develop a positive sense of self and a zest for living in an ever-changing and challenging world. Without doubt, these benefits contribute to academic success, as well, in such areas as science, mathematics, early literacy, social studies, and the arts.

Some adults, aware of the value of play to child development and learning, have a tendency to organize and plan play sessions for children. Adults set the agendas and direct the activities. They often introduce "games with rules" (board games, bowling, tag, etc.) and provide materials that are designed to be used in a narrowly-specified way (puzzles, bingo, matching games, etc.). While such activities and materials have a place in child development, they should not be used instead of creative play. In creative play, children set the agenda (or play around with no agenda) and choose their own materials. They set their own rules (or decide there are no rules) and use open-ended materials (materials that can be used in a wide variety of ways).

The emphasis of this book is on creative play – the type of play that is so engaging and valuable for children but troublesome for some adults. Adults may feel that children are just wasting time during creative play. After all, what could they be learning by filling a bucket with sand, pouring it out, and refilling it again – especially if they do this over and over again? As will become evident through the discussions in this book, children can be learning a lot by just "messing around" with simple materials.

This book is primarily about creative play in an outdoor environment. Making an argument for the out-of-doors as a natural place for children to play was unnecessary for most adults of previous generations. The outdoors was "the place" to play. When children became restless indoors or were "underfoot" as parents tried to get some work done, children were often told to "go outside and play." And children needed little coaxing. There was so much to do in the out-of-doors – explore creek beds, watch (or chase) butterflies and lightning bugs, build dens in the woods, load stones in a bucket, and "plant a garden" of twigs. This type of play was freely chosen, engaged the senses, involved problem-solving and imagination, and motivated children to take risks. This is the type of play that will be encouraged throughout this book and will be referred to as "creative play."

While creative play can and does occur in almost any environment, recent research indicates that natural outdoor spaces have a special quality that promotes the frequency, duration, and quality of creative play (Bilton 2010a, Elliot 2008, Louv 2006). Natural outdoor playspaces are spaces that have trees, grass, and other types of vegetation. They also feature a variety of natural materials for children to manipulate, such as stones, leaves, and twigs.

Creative play in natural environments is encouraged for the benefits it offers to children, the natural world, and society at large. Some of the benefits to children have already been discussed in relation to developmental and academic outcomes. To these, we can add benefits relating to children's spiritual life, as connections with nature often inspire a sense of wonder and awe – and, at times, even a sense of the sacred or sublime (Schein 2011). For the natural world, the benefits of creative play in natural environments include the development of deeper understandings and appreciation of nature. These understandings and values lead to care and protection of the natural world (Orr 2004). For society, creative play in natural environments can foster empathy, perspective taking, sensitivity to life, insights into interdependence, and the development of a more peaceful and sustainable world (Mische and Harris 2008).

This book is designed to promote the healthy development of children and an ethic of caring for the environment. While some may think that a more efficient way of promoting an environmental ethic would be through direct teaching, research and theory in the fields of early childhood education and environmental education do not support the direct-teaching approach (Copple and Bredekamp 2009, NAAEE 2010).

From the early childhood education literature, we know that young children construct their own knowledge and build a sense of "rightness" and responsibility from the inside out – versus having knowledge and ethics handed to them from the outside. And from the environmental education literature, we know that environmental stewardship is rooted in a sense of appreciation and caring. Fear and mandates have not been effective in developing strong commitments to protecting the environment. Early positive experiences in natural environments have proven to be a far more effective way of fostering environmental stewardship (Chawla and Hart 1995). Thus, the ideas for creative play presented in this book focus on outdoor playspaces that give young children a variety of rich opportunities to interact with the natural world. While one chapter (Chapter 3) is devoted to the indoor environment, the focus remains on learning about the natural world through direct interactions with natural materials – that is, of finding ways to "bring the outdoors in."

Some may wonder if *Nature and Young Children* is an early childhood education book or an environmental education book. It is, in fact, both, as it promotes the goals of each of these disciplines. In relation to early childhood education, the focus is on holistic development of the young child. In relation to environmental education, the focus is on learning in, for, about, and *from* the natural world. This focus represents an expanded definition of how environmental education is traditionally defined – that is "education in, for, and about the environment." The expanded definition proposed here recognizes that nature itself is a teacher. From nature, we learn about systems and interdependence; about diversity and the way in which it enriches the environment; about beauty and mystery and the role these play in our lives; about life and death, adaptation, interconnectedness, patterns, and cycles. From nature, we also learn about ourselves as being a part of and dependent upon something greater than ourselves.

Chapter 1 presents arguments from research and theory as to why children need time in the out-of-doors and opportunities to interact with the natural environment. The discussion in this chapter explains how interactions with nature benefit young children in all areas of development (physical, emotional, cognitive, social, aesthetic, etc.), while also promoting a positive environmental ethic. The ideas of creative play and a sense of wonder are also discussed.

Chapter 2 presents ideas and guidelines for designing natural outdoor playspaces for young children. Design considerations include attention to desired outcomes and the quality of children's experiences while engaged in outdoor play. Related topics focus on the value of outdoor learning centers, a variety of play zones, and the availability of loose parts. This chapter also includes design criteria for environmental yards and a checklist for evaluating outdoor environments for young children.

Chapter 3 addresses ways in which the indoor classroom can be used to promote an understanding and appreciation of the natural environment. Specific ideas on how "to bring the outdoors in" include adding natural materials to the learning centers, making animals and plants a part of the indoor environment, and introducing pro-nature books to children.

The role of the adult in making outdoor play creative and meaningful for young children is discussed in Chapter 4. The focus is on how adults can support children's play and learning activities in a non-instructive and non-intrusive way. Specific guidelines and suggestions are provided as to what to do and what not to do in promoting a variety of creative play and learning activities in the out-of-doors.

Chapter 5 discusses how creative play in natural environments can foster the holistic development of young children in the different developmental domains: adaptive, aesthetic, cognitive, social, emotional, and physical. This chapter also addresses the importance of wonder, creativity, and imagination to the holistic development of children and ways in which play in natural environments can foster each of these areas. New to this second edition is a brief discussion about the spiritual development of children and how it is fostered through positive connections with nature.

Chapter 6 presents ideas on how interacting with the natural environment can foster specific understandings and skills in the academic areas of literacy, mathematics, science, social studies, and art and music. Also presented is an activity/learning grid indicating how one activity can meet multiple goals across academic areas. This grid, as well as the chapter summary, reinforces the idea of thinking of curriculum at the early childhood level as being integrated versus divided into discrete academic areas.

Chapter 7 focuses specifically on the development of conservation attitudes and a positive ecological identity through nature play activities. Emphasis is placed on dispositions and attitudes relating to empathy, caring, and perspective taking. Related topics addressed in this chapter include biophilia, biophobia, and place-based learning, as these relate to the development of conservation attitudes.

Chapter 8 addresses some special considerations that teachers, parents, and other adults may have about connecting young children with nature. These considerations include (1) accessibility for *all* children, including children with disabilities; (2) technology in the lives of children; and (3) cultural sensitivity.

An epilogue – new to this second edition – presents a brief discussion on how creative play in natural environments can contribute to the creation of a more peaceful society. Following this are two appendices – one describing a few exceptional natural playspaces for young children and the other presenting selected resources, including a *Nurturing Nature and Young Children Index* designed to serve as a tool for evaluating an early childhood program in relation to the major principles outlined in this book. The last section of this book also includes a list of references and a topical index.

Many aspects of society today (computers, TV, crime, the preponderance of cars, etc.) separate children from nature and suggest that "nature is something to watch, to consume, to wear – to ignore" (Louv 2006: 2). Adults who care about children and the natural environment are called upon to consciously and thoughtfully find ways to bring nature back into children's lives. Unless we do this, children will miss out on a critical aspect of childhood. Ultimately, separation from the natural world will also diminish the richness of the human experience and our ability to be good stewards of the natural world. Let's not allow this to be the fate of future generations; let's give young children natural places to play, to learn, to wonder, and to experience joy.

# 1 Nature play

Think of nature and think of play. Combine the two. That's nature play! For adults, nature play might be kayaking on a river or lake, climbing a mountain, planting peas, or walking barefoot on a sandy beach. For a young child, nature play might be making mud pies, digging in the sand, running through a pile of leaves, or floating leaves and bark in a bucket of water.

Nature play is not just any type of outdoor play, as nature play involves playing *with* nature, not just *in* nature (Erickson and Ernst 2011). For young children, nature play represents a remarkable "goodness of fit" (Wilson 2010a), as the characteristics of young children mesh extremely well with the play potential of natural environments and natural materials. Nature invites authentic play – the best kind of play for young children! Authentic play is fun, open-ended, self-directed, and freely chosen (Miller *et al.* 2009, Stephens 2009). Authentic play occurs naturally when children and nature are brought together.

While we often think of nature play as occurring outdoors, this type of play can take place indoors, as well. The outdoor environment tends to offer more opportunities for active engagement with nature, but natural materials can be brought indoors to provide another setting for nature play. Think of it as "bringing the outdoors in." It's unfortunate that our lives in today's society tend to have clear divisions (walls) between indoors and out. It hasn't always been this way; and with a little imagination, we can find creative ways to invite more of nature – and hands-on interactions with nature – into our indoor spaces.

In a review of the research on nature play, Erickson and Ernst (2011) identified the following benefits:

- Nature play makes kids healthier by stimulating higher levels of physical activity.
- Nature play makes kids smarter by boosting brain development.

- Nature play makes kids feel better by fostering emotional well–being and strengthening social bonds.
- Nature play is good for the Earth by preconditioning children to care about the natural world later in life.

Presented in Box 1.1 is a brief overview of nature play. Further discussion about nature play and young children is presented in the following sections of this chapter.

**Box 1.1** Ins and outs of nature play

## What's nature play?

Think of nature and think of play. Combine the two. That's nature play! For adults, nature play might be kayaking on a river or lake, climbing a mountain, planting peas, or walking barefoot on a sandy beach. For a young child, nature play might be making mud pies, digging in the sand, running through a pile of leaves, or floating leaves and bark in a bucket of water.

## What makes nature play authentic?

To be authentic, nature play must involve natural materials; and for the young child, it should be fun, self-directed, and freely chosen.

## Can nature play take place indoors?

Yes! Nature play can take place both indoors and outdoors. The outdoor environment tends to offer more opportunities for active engagement with nature, but natural materials can be brought indoors to provide another setting for nature play.

## What's good about nature play?

Nature play helps us make positive connections with nature, and that's good for us and good for the environment. For us, there are physical, emotional, mental, and spiritual benefits. For the environment, nature play fosters love for nature which leads to wanting to take care of the environment.

## What's special about nature play for young children?

There's a natural connection – or a "goodness of fit" – between young children and nature. Play is the most effective way for young children to learn about themselves and the world around them. Combining nature and play in the lives of young children has many benefits. Some of these benefits are:

- increased sense of wonder and imagination;
- increased observational skills and curiosity;
- improved awareness and ability to concentrate;

- increased joy and confidence;
- enhanced social skills and self-efficacy;
- increased problem-solving and critical thinking skills;
- increased interest in and concern for the environment.

## What are the rules for nature play?

The rules for nature play are not like the rules for soft ball or tag. As nature play is self-directed, the only rules for this kind of play have to do with safety and respect: (a) be safe; (b) respect others; and (c) respect the environment. To help children understand these rules, we can remind them to:

- ask an adult before eating anything they find outdoors;
- be kind and helpful to each other;
- take care of plants and other living things;
- put trash in trash containers;
- recycle what they can;
- use only what they need (don't waste paper and water).

## What are some great ways to facilitate nature play?

The best way to facilitate nature play is to let children play outside in a natural environment. Support their play by providing a variety of loose parts and play props, by showing interest and offering encouragement, and letting them direct their own play.

For indoor nature play, provide a variety of natural materials and related play props. Encourage children to make natural materials a part of their art experiences and use nature-related ideas as themes for pretend play.

## Children and childhood

Nature play comes naturally to young children in situations where children and childhood are understood and respected. A child, as defined by the dictionary (*The American Heritage*, fourth edition), is "a person between birth and puberty; an immature person." Anyone who actually spends time with children realizes that this definition of a child is fundamentally shallow and incomplete.

Children are busy people. They like to touch, taste, poke, dig, tear, shake, pull, push, and climb. They're curious and eager to follow the path of curiosity. They're observant and imaginative – often seeing patterns, shapes, and possibilities that adults rarely notice. Children are intense, sensitive, and highly competent. They're also philosophical and spiritual (Hart 2005, Wilson 2010b).

Many adults overlook the uniqueness of childhood. They accept the dictionary definition of a child and view the years of childhood as a "transition" period – a time devoted to waiting for the child to mature into an adult. Adults with this view believe it's their job to prepare children for what they will face in the future. Such adults fail to acknowledge the importance of valuing children for who they really are and the years of childhood as a special time in the lives of individuals.

We live in an achievement-oriented society with an intense focus on what should be accomplished for the sake of the future. This orientation – along with the mistaken idea of childhood – leads to the misguided introduction of formal academic instruction at an early age and high-stakes testing soon after children enter school. These well-intentioned initiatives place a great deal of stress on children and compromise their emotional well-being (Crain 2003). A number of studies indicate that children's academic and social development is also compromised when they are subjected to pressures and expectations not appropriate to their age (Bredekamp and Copple 1997, Elkind 1987).

## Creative play

An appreciation of nature play requires an understanding of the value of creative play in the life of a young child. In addition to love and protection, what young children most need is the time, place, and materials to engage in authentic play. It's through play that children learn about themselves and the world around them. It's through play that they develop a sense of competence and make invaluable discoveries about their social, cultural, and physical environments. Most of what children need to learn during their early childhood years cannot be taught; it's discovered through play.

Some adults, however, view play as having little value. They're concerned when children spend too much time "just playing." They may view pretend play as cute or charming, but not as educationally serious as learning to read and write. Adults sometimes wonder: "Aren't children just wasting their time when engaged in pretend play? Shouldn't they be learning about the 'real' versus 'imaginary' world?" The answer is a resounding *no*!

The imaginary world of children helps them learn many critical concepts about the world that we call "real." An essential concept embedded in pretend play is the understanding that one thing can represent something else. A stick can be a magic wand; small stones can be birds' eggs; and the children, themselves, can be veterinarians or wildlife photographers. At first glance, this may not seem significant. Yet, the underlying concepts behind such essential skills as reading, writing, drawing, map making, understanding and expressing ideas, and planning for the future involve our ability to make something stand for (or represent) something else. This ability – so readily developed through creative play – is crucial for later academic success. Children who can readily manipulate symbols in dramatic play are more likely to accept and use the symbols associated with mathematics, reading, and writing (Bilton 2010b, National Arbor Day Foundation 2007).

We can't teach the concept of representation – children need to discover and experiment with it on their own. Creative play is the appropriate medium for developing this understanding during the early childhood years.

Children gain other concepts and skills as they play, as well. They use their senses, explore their environment, solve problems, and then incorporate what they experience into their internal system of thought. Play also promotes children's social and emotional development. As they play, children learn to share, cooperate, take turns, and negotiate. As they play with others, children experience different personalities, temperaments, and ways of doing things, and – in the process – gain valuable insights into themselves and each other. Through role play, children are able to "decenter" – to get into another person's shoes and to see things from another perspective (Bilton 2002).

Both self-concept and self-esteem are also fostered through creative play, as play helps children learn about their bodies, their abilities, and their relationships with others. They learn to deal with frustrations, to make decisions, and to challenge themselves in social, cognitive, and physical activities. They also learn to help each other. During pretend peer play, children help each other concentrate and stay within a character's boundaries (Stephens 2009). If a child is pretending to be a dog, for example, he or she must stay in "dog character." Children often remind each other how to do this.

Play is an "easy means of learning for young children, as they are naturally drawn to it and want to get involved in it" (Bilton 2002: 116). Because they find play motivating, children will often exercise great self-control and cooperation with the group so as not to stop or spoil a play situation.

Play also fosters the physical health and development of children. During play, large muscles are exercised; balance, coordination, and endurance are strengthened; and small muscle skills are refined. Active play also helps prevent obesity.

The National Association for the Education of Young Children (NAEYC) (Copple and Bredekamp 2009) states that children should be given ample opportunities to play because of the many benefits it offers. Following are some of the benefits outlined by NAEYC:

- Play is an active form of learning that unites the mind, body, and spirit.
- Play reduces the tension that often comes with expectations to achieve.
- Play provides a healthy avenue for expressing and working out emotional aspects of everyday experiences.
- Play helps children develop the ability to see things from another person's point of view.
- Play engages all the senses as powerful modes of learning.
- Play helps children gain competence in moving through the larger world.

It's important for parents and teachers to demonstrate a positive attitude towards imaginative play. Children should never be criticized or discouraged from engaging in pretend play. One child pretending to be a dolphin was reprimanded by a teacher for "acting silly." Even if it was time to move on to a different activity (e.g. lunch, dismissal, etc.), the child's play should not have been labeled "silly." The teacher could have responded in a more appropriate way by saying something like: "Dion, you have some interesting ideas about dolphins. Maybe you can show me some more of your ideas tomorrow. Right now, it's time to wash your hands for lunch."

Some parents and teachers make another mistake. They notice what a child is doing during creative play and then try to take over the play scenario. Their intentions are to extend the child's learning – to add more information (facts), more learning outcomes for the child. The adult mistakenly thinks this will increase the richness of the learning episode. There are times when the adult's participation in a child's creative play activity does lead to enhanced learning, but this rarely occurs when the adult takes the "directing role" away from a child. The adult's attitudes and behaviors should leave the child feeling that he or she is a competent, interesting, and creative individual. Taking over a child-initiated activity does not give children this positive message. While the adult can introduce some props and ideas, the child should be allowed to remain in the role of director – especially for dramatic play and other creative activities.

The UN Convention on the Rights of the Child recognizes the right to play as one of the basic rights of children. As stated in Article 31 of the Convention, children have the right "to rest and leisure, to engage in play and recreational activities appropriate to the age of the child." It is up to adults to protect and support this right for children.

## The natural environment

The natural environment is an ideal place for children to engage in creative play. The following statements by Greenman (2005) help to explain why nature is so rich in play potential:

- Nature is universal and timeless.
- Nature is unpredictable.
- Nature is bountiful.
- Nature is beautiful.
- Nature is alive with sounds.
- Nature creates a multitude of places.
- Nature is real.
- Nature nourishes and heals.

The UN Convention on the Rights of the Child also recognizes the right of children to live and play in an environment that stimulates their healthy development. Natural environments stimulate play, development, and learning in a special boundless way. Nature must, therefore, be seen as an essential component of the children's environment (Moore and Cosco 2006).

While children find ways to play anywhere with almost anything, some environments and materials are more conducive to creative play than others – that is, they have more play potential or play value. Studies of children in different types of environments indicate that children engage in more creative forms of play (including fantasy and pretend play) in "green" or "natural" areas than in more traditional playgrounds or "prepared" indoor playspaces (Elliot 2008, Louv 2006, Moore and Cosco 2006).

Bilton's (2002) summary of research comparing indoor and outdoor play outlines some additional relevant findings. These findings indicate that some children

- are socially more inhibited when indoors;
- benefit from a higher level of learning when outdoors;

- are more assertive outdoors;
- concentrate longer outdoors; and – not surprisingly –
- prefer to play outdoors.

Findings also indicate that pretend play tends to be the most dominant form of play outside. Bilton (2002) explains this by noting that what the outdoors affords to young children is the opportunity to be in role, to be playing imaginatively, and enables them to be involved in fairly large groups. This is not only because there is more space, and noise is more easily dissipated outside, but also because there is a greater sense of freedom in the outdoors.

## Children and nature

Unless influenced otherwise, young children are fascinated by the natural world. They're drawn to other living things, especially animals. They reach out to pick flowers, to put their hands in water and sand, and to dig for natural treasures in a mound of dirt. Evidence suggests that children also know and experience the natural world differently from adults (Bilton 2010b, Sebba 1991). According to Rachel Carson (1956: 42), the child knows the world as being "fresh and new and beautiful, full of wonder and excitement." As for adults, Carson (1956: 42) says: "It is our misfortune that for most of us that clear-eyed vision, that true instinct for what is beautiful and awe-inspiring, is dimmed and even lost before we reach adulthood."

Some people are surprised to learn that Carson wrote about children and nature. They know Rachel Carson primarily as a scientist who ushered in the environmental movement with her research and writings on the dangers of pesticides to the natural world. As a scientist, Carson spent a great deal of time in close, objective observation of the physical world around her. But – as reflected in the quote above – Carson also thought about children and their unique way of experiencing the world. She placed great value on children's way of knowing and the impact of nature as a source of wonder and delight. She advocated frequent opportunities for children to walk in the woods and along the water's edge in all kinds of weather. And she recognized (through her excursions with her nephew, Roger) that children – even as young infants – possess an acceptance of a world of "elemental things" and that they find great joy and delight in experiencing and exploring the natural world.

Others who have compared children's experience of the world to that of adults include Rachel Sebba and Joseph Clinton Pearce. According to Sebba (1991), children perceive the world through the gift of "primal seeing." This gift allows them to experience the "magic" or "essence" of the world around them. Pearce (1992) describes children's way of knowing the world in similar terms. He talks about "magical thinking" and "primary perceptions" during the years of childhood. While this way of knowing or seeing the world differs from the adult's, it should not be viewed as incorrect or inferior. In fact, it would be well – that is, respectful of children and promoting their holistic development – for parents and other adults to honor and celebrate children's way of knowing the world and give them ample opportunities for playing and exploring in a natural environment.

Young children not only know the world differently from adults, they also do different things in interacting with nature. The natural world for children is not just a scene or backdrop – it's something to be interacted with. Young children want to do more than look. They want to touch, dig, poke, shake, pound, pour, smell, taste, and "muck around." They want to explore and experiment. They want to be busy doing something – and it is through such busyness that they learn about the natural world and about themselves. Both research and theory strongly support the idea of young children "learning through doing" in the form of creative play (Copple and Bredekamp 2009).

Many children today are deprived of frequent positive experiences with the natural world. Researchers and child development specialists are beginning to study the causes and consequences of this situation. Richard Louv (2006), in *The Last Child in the Woods: Saving Our Children from Nature-Deficit Disorder*, uses the term "de-naturing of childhood" and discusses its extent, possible causes, and impact. He talks about the "criminalization of natural play," which he views as both a symptom and cause of the move from children living immersed in the natural world to being divorced from that world.

Louv notes that the "de-naturing of childhood" can be attributed to various conditions – some that are cultural or institutional, others that are personal or familial. Cultural and institutional barriers include the growing practice of litigation, trends in education that marginalize direct experience in nature, and the structure of cities. Personal or familial barriers include time pressures and fear. Many parents are caught up in the "waste no time" syndrome. They feel that to get ahead, children's lives should be carefully programmed. Thus, from early on, they enroll their children in such activities as competitive sports, computer camps, and other types of "enrichment activities" (dance, art and music lessons, "early science," etc.). They also pressure their children to excel in school – with the emphasis on high grades and test scores. "Just playing" in this get-ahead culture, Louv notes, is considered a waste of valuable time.

When children are given time to play, it's often in a commercialized or computerized environment. Indoor play centers are becoming increasingly popular – video arcades, "water baby" swimming pools, and climbing structures in shopping malls. Even some nature centers and parks are beginning to develop elaborate indoor exhibits and classrooms – some of which include climbing walls, artificial trees, and computer games.

"Entertainment" for children often replaces creative play – for example, TVs and DVD players in children's bedrooms, computers and entertainment centers in family rooms, family outings to movie theaters and organized sports events. While these forms of entertainment may not be harmful in themselves, they erode the time and freedom children have for creative play. And this is a problem, as children need creative play to develop in a holistic way. Creative play can't be hurried or tightly scheduled between completing homework and getting ready for swimming lessons.

Too much time in commercialized and computerized environments not only deprives children of time to play, but it also separates them from nature. This is a problem, as children need nature – not something to study or look at, but to interact with. And as Louv (2006: 117) says: "It takes time – loose, unstructured dreamtime – to experience nature in a meaningful way."

## Play in natural environments

Young children's way of knowing and learning makes them excellent candidates for nature exploration. Such explorations foster the child's health, ability to concentrate, and emotional bonding with the natural world (Elliot 2008, Erickson and Ernst 2011). The natural world offers an incredible wealth of sensory experiences and open-ended materials for motoric manipulation. Experiences in natural outdoor playspaces also tend to be rich in opportunities for nurturing growth in all areas of child development (Miller *et al.* 2009). Another advantage of play in a natural environment is the lessening of aggressive behaviors and accidents. Children tend to bridge their differences more easily in a natural environment; fights and accidents – so common on asphalt yards – give way to more constructive play (Hines 2005).

The quality of play also tends to be richer in natural versus "prepared" environments. Studies comparing play in green, natural spaces with play in blacktop playgrounds found that play on asphalt was much more interrupted and consisted of short segments. In more natural areas, on the other hand, children were more likely to invent whole sagas that they carried from day to day. Natural schoolyards encouraged more fantasy and make-believe play, and provided ways for boys and girls to play together in egalitarian ways. Children playing in more natural areas also showed a greater sense of wonder (Louv 2006).

Researchers who have contributed to our understanding of the value of play in natural environments include Edward O. Wilson and Howard Gardner. Wilson (1984), a scientist at Harvard University, suggests that humans have an innate affinity for the

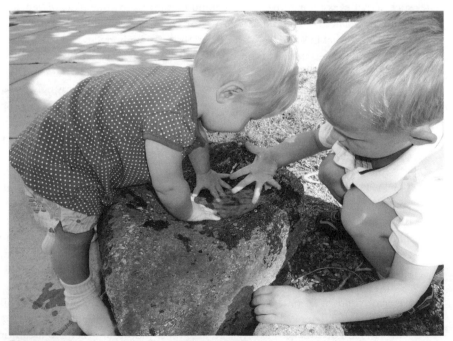

**Photograph 1.1**　Nature play with water and rock

natural world. He introduced the term "biophilia" and described it as "the urge to affiliate with other forms of life." He and his colleagues proposed that biophilia is biologically based and integral to our development as individuals. The concept of biophilia suggests that play in natural environments matches an innate need of young children and fosters their holistic development.

Howard Gardner, a professor of education at Harvard University, also recognizes the value of involvement with nature to child development. In the early 1980s, Gardner raised the idea of expanding our traditional understanding of human intelligence. He suggested that results of an IQ test provide far too limited a view of one's intelligence and introduced the idea of multiple intelligences. He originally proposed seven types of intelligence: linguistic, logical-mathematical, spatial, bodily-kinesthetic, musical, interpersonal, and intrapersonal. He has since added the idea of an eighth intelligence – that is, the naturalistic intelligence. The core of this intelligence, he says, is the ability to recognize plants, animals, and other parts of the natural environment. It also deals with sensing patterns in and making connections to elements in the natural world (Gardner 1999). Gardner suggested that Rachel Carson clearly manifested a naturalistic intelligence.

Children with a strong naturalistic intelligence may exhibit some or all of the following:

- keen sensory skills (sight, sound, smell, taste, and touch);
- tendency to notice and categorize elements of the natural world;
- enjoy being outdoors and engaging in such nature-related activities as gardening, exploring natural areas, and observing natural phenomena (e.g. movement of clouds, singing of birds, effects of wind and rain, etc.);
- easily notice patterns in their natural surroundings (differences, similarities, linkages, etc.);
- an interest in and caring about animals and plants;
- enjoy collecting nature-related specimens (e.g. leaves, rocks, shells, seeds, etc.);
- awareness of and concern for the well-being of the natural world;
- easily learn new information about natural objects and species, and understand ecological concepts.

According to Gardner's theory (1999), everyone has each type of intelligence to varying degrees, but culture and experience play a role in the development of a particular type of intelligence. Each type of intelligence needs a related stimulating physical and social environment to maximize its development.

Creative play in natural environments allows the naturalistic intelligence to flourish. The core of learning about the natural environment is not embedded in information provided to a child (knowledge presented from the outside) but in the interaction between the child and the world of nature. This approach to learning is sometimes referred to as environment-based or place-based education and is characterized by direct experiences with nature (Louv 2006, Sobel 2004a). "The basic idea [of place-based education] is to use the surrounding community, including nature, as the preferred classroom" (Louv 2006: 204). This approach has proven effective – not only in fostering the naturalistic intelligence but also in improving academic performance (Louv 2006, Sobel 2004b).

Adults can help children develop the naturalistic intelligence by encouraging them to collect natural materials (seeds, stones, leaves, flowers, etc.), closely observe the different types of plants and animals in their yard and community park, study books and magazines with pictures of plants and animals, and engage in nature-related activities, such as gardening, hiking, climbing, exploring, etc.

## Related educational models

The idea of connecting children with nature is not new to early childhood education. Educators, in both formal settings (schools) and non-formal settings (e.g. children's museums), have been using nature as a topic, context, and motivation for learning over the years. Today, however, the use of computers, videos, educational TV, other commercially packaged materials, and an emphasis on testing based on "book learning" have greatly diminished the extent to which children and nature are connected through educational programs.

The theory and research behind some educational models provide support for a return to closer linkages with the natural environment. Such models are based on the understanding that young children and nature have much in common. Both grow better when carefully nurtured and both engender a sense of joy and excitement.

Froebel, the founder of the kindergarten movement, suggested a "children's garden" as the most appropriate setting for the education of young children, and the curriculum that he developed was based on the child's inherent need to play. Froebel's ideas were radical for his day (Wellhousen 2002). According to Froebel, the outdoor environment and activities should be as carefully planned and implemented as those indoors and both should focus on children's interaction with the natural world. Froebel encouraged the planting and watering of seeds, frequent nature walks where children and their teacher could explore the natural world together, and a variety of loose materials that allow children to build and experiment.

The Reggio Emilia approach to education is another model that weds children and the environment. In fact, one of the guiding principles of this approach is the understanding that the environment serves "as a third teacher" (Ceppi and Zini 1998). Both the indoor and outdoor environments are carefully considered and constructed, with the use of natural materials being emphasized throughout. The use of natural materials is seen in the decoration of the room and in the materials available for investigation and creativity. Long, uninterrupted periods of time outdoors are also provided to allow for child-directed exploration and play.

Other educational theorists advocating learning outdoors in natural settings include Dewey, Rousseau and Montessori. Their philosophies are based on the understanding that the natural world is one of the best resources for educating children and for nurturing their spirits. Unfortunately, many early childhood programs today reflect a very different focus, with an emphasis on abstract and vicarious versus concrete and first-hand learning experiences.

But people are getting concerned. After the publication of Richard Louv's book, *The Last Child in the Woods* (2006), we're seeing an international movement to get kids outdoors – not just for recreation, but also for education. Educators and other adults concerned about children *and* the environment are asking, "How can children learn about and develop a caring relationship with nature without spending time outside?" The Children and Nature Network (C&NN) and the Nature Action Collaborative for Children (NACC) represent two rapidly-growing organizations focusing on connecting children with nature. See Appendix 2 for a brief description of these two organizations.

## Sense of wonder

We sometimes talk about the "gifts of nature" – what an apt description of what nature offers to human development and enjoyment of life! Philosophers, psychologists, and nature writers often use this term in describing how nature lifts and inspires us (Kaplan and Kaplan 1989). We also see that nature fosters creativity and imagination, as so much of art is inspired by the beauty and mystery of the natural world. For many, nature soothes and comforts, as well. People often turn to nature when stressed or confused. A special place by the sea, under a tree, or in a garden helps many of us find a sense of peace. Children experience similar gifts of comfort, calm, and peace when engaged with nature (Elliot 2008).

Rachel Carson speaks of another gift, as well – the gift of a sense of wonder. Carson believes that children have an inborn sense of wonder that can serve "as an unfailing antidote against the boredom and disenchantments of later years, the sterile preoccupation with things that are artificial, the alienation from the sources of our strength" (Carson 1956: 43). To keep this sense of wonder alive, children need frequent opportunities to play freely and creatively in natural outdoor playspaces that are rich in beauty and variety. They need soul-enriching experiences to grow into the fullness of what it means to be human. It is through the medium of the natural world that they are most likely to encounter such experiences. Among other things, nature-related experiences foster the child's emerging sense of wonder, which is one of the primary sources of knowledge. In fact, some philosophers and educational psychologists contend that it is only through wonder that we can come to know the world as it really is (Cobb 1977).

# Natural outdoor playspaces

The cultivation of flowers and trees is the cultivation of the good, the beautiful, and the ennobling in man.

(J. Sterling Morton, founder of Arbor Day)

We often use the term "playgrounds" when we talk about outdoor areas designed specifically for young children. Unfortunately, many such playspaces fail to foster creative play and are often devoid of "ground" (i.e. soil), as well – thus, making the term "playgrounds" an inaccurate description of what's offered. Traditionally, playgrounds feature "equipment" – swings, slides, and climbing structures. The surface of many playgrounds consists of asphalt. Such playspaces fall miserably short in addressing the holistic needs of children. Children need more than equipment; they need opportunities to explore, experiment, manipulate, create, and learn about the natural world. Children also need environments that tell them that they are competent and respected. They need playspaces that put them in touch with beauty, arouse their curiosity, and excite their imaginations. There's a reason why children prefer to "play under the bushes" (Wilson 2004) rather than use traditional playground equipment. This reason has a lot to do with children's need to make a playspace their own. Playground equipment is usually cemented or bolted in one place and cannot be rearranged by children. Another disadvantage of playground equipment is its lack of transferability – it's designed to be used in a prescribed way instead of offering options for how to use it.

Lack of transferability greatly limits the play potential or play value of equipment and materials. Several research studies focusing on different types of enclosures or "dens" reinforce this concept. Elliot (2008), in reporting on this research, notes that play in child-constructed enclosures was "more sustained, complex and creative" than in adult-constructed enclosures. The adult-constructed enclosures were usually built with uniform materials (e.g. boards of a consistent texture and pre-determined lengths) and tended to have just one entrance and exit point (a door with hinges). Such enclosures reflect a single purpose – playing house – and are usually equipped with adult-chosen props (small table and chairs, toy dishes, etc.).

Child-constructed enclosures, on the other hand, were built with whatever was at hand – such as branches, logs, leaves, and a large piece of cloth – and were used for a variety of play purposes (e.g. pretending to be animals in a den, camping in the woods, having a secret hide-out, etc.). Child-built enclosures usually had multiple entrance and exit points, allowing for more movement and inviting more imagination. Children playing in the child-constructed enclosures used a variety of self-selected natural materials as play props, and seemed to enjoy the sense of control they had over their play setting.

Children crave choice, challenge, and the opportunity to exercise their imagination. On playgrounds that offer only simple fixed play units, children have a tendency to add risk and challenge in order to cope with the limited choices afforded by the equipment. They will jump from high places, go backwards down the slide, and find other ways of testing the limits of people and materials in a play setting that offers few options for creativity.

In addition to safety concerns associated with such "testing the limits," there are other shortcomings to the standard playground consisting of swings, slides, and see-saws. This traditional design cannot provide the appropriate opportunities to meet the changing needs of developing children.

Dramatic play and exploration of the natural environment aren't fostered on the standard playground. The design of the playground tends to direct children to gross motor activities and fails to provide the necessary materials to stimulate other types of activities. Play in such an environment doesn't spiral upwards in complexity, thus seriously limiting the learning potential. This limitation influences children's behavior in a negative way. On playgrounds where equipment is the only option for play, children tend to become aggressive and bored, and rarely engage in creative or cooperative play. An equipment-only playground sets the stage for quarreling and limited positive experiences for many of the children while outdoors (Nicolson and Shipstead 2002).

## What children need and want

Children need playspaces that are designed with their needs and interests in mind. In fact, in planning an outdoor playspace, children's ideas should be solicited and taken seriously. When asked during the planning stage of one garden about what they would like best, the most common responses from children (from two to twelve years of age) included a waterfall, a pond with fish and frogs, animals, and sweet-tasting fruits and vegetables. They also suggested scarecrows, trees to climb, and flowers to pick (Hefferman 1994). When another group of children were asked what would make their neighborhood a better place for kids, their responses (as published by Peace Child International 1992) included:

- "I think kids should have a garden all their own where there are no 'do not touch' signs."

- "I would like a place where the sky is blue, the air is clean, birds sing, the sun is shining, the earth is covered with rich forests, and everything around smells of strawberries."
- "I would like a tree house, but one that I can get in" (comment made by a girl with a physical disability).

Unfortunately, the role of the physical environment is to a large extent not even considered – nor is it clearly understood as a dynamic part of the supporting environment – when playspaces for children are being designed (Cosco and Moore 2006). This is especially true of the outdoor environment. In fact, in many instances the outdoor playspace may be the most neglected area of early childhood programs.

Some playgrounds are actually bad for children – they are developmentally sterile, and they are hazardous. Many traditional playgrounds are dangerous to the health and safety of young children and serious injuries occur far too often. Such injuries include broken bones, concussion, brain damage, and sometimes even result in death.

## Special places

A growing cadre of individuals has been working to call attention to the importance of quality outdoor playspaces for young children that include access to nature. These individuals are motivated by a concern for children's holistic development and a concern for the way humans relate to the natural environment. Thus, "special places" are being designed with the welfare of children and the environment in mind. Some such playspaces are referred to as "environmental yards," "children's gardens," and "natural habitats for children." Other "special places" for children involve little or no "designing" or construction by adults. They're natural places left in their natural state. Forest kindergartens are good examples of this.

A forest kindergarten is a school in the forest where educational activities are held almost entirely in a natural outdoor setting. Forest kindergartens usually serve children between the ages of three and six, and focus on building positive connections with the natural environment. Materials used in a forest kindergarten are primarily natural materials versus commercially made "educational materials." For example, leaves and other plant materials are used to "paint" a picture or make a collage; and sticks versus blocks are used to build a road or make a bridge.

The term for forest kindergarten in German is "*waldkindergartens*," with "*waldkinder*" meaning "children of the forest." While forest kindergartens are becoming popular in Europe, there are only a few in the United States. One such program is highlighted in Appendix 1, along with other "special places" for young children.

"*Naturebornehaver*" (nature nursery school) is the Scandinavian term for forest kindergarten. Children participating in a *naturebornehaver* spend their time playing in woodlands and meadows. The focus of the curriculum is not academic. The emphasis is on free play, creativity, socialization, and emotional stability (Knight 2009). Getting children out in nature for extended periods of time in different seasons and in all kinds of weather fits the cultural norms of Scandinavia. As Scandinavian attitudes about children and risk taking tend to be more liberal than in some other countries, it is not unusual to find young children in a *naturebornehaver* program climbing very high in trees, whittling sticks with knives, and cooking food over open fires (Knight 2009).

In the United Kingdom, "forest schools" (the term used for forest kindergartens in the United Kingdom) were first established in the early 1990s. Related research indicated that these schools were effective in fostering students' self-esteem, confidence, and well-being. In some cases, the effect on individual children is dramatic. Knight (2009) reports seeing an anxious four-year-old – afraid to even try to balance on a log at the beginning of the program – running along a log with confidence to reach a tree to climb by Week 10. Knight also witnessed a child with a speech impairment find her voice and confidence to express her extraordinary storytelling skills in the woods. Additional benefits of the forest schools included marked improvements in concentration, perseverance, cooperation, and motivation (Knight 2009). Based in part on this convincing research, the Early Years Foundation Stage curriculum (the governmental statutory curriculum framework for the care and education of children aged 0–5 in early childhood settings in England) now requires all settings to recognize the importance of outdoor learning for young children. The Forestry Commission is also committed to supporting forest schools throughout the whole of the United Kingdom (Knight 2009).

## Design considerations

An educationally sound way to start planning learning environments for young children is to ask what we want children to learn and/or experience in such environments. Following is a list of desired outcomes for outdoor environments based on work published by Ceppi and Zini (1998), Greenman (2005), and Wellhousen (2002):

- experience new physical challenges;
- develop strength and stamina;
- use large muscles and fine muscles in new ways;
- engage in problem-solving;
- interact with peers by talking and playing;
- appreciate nature and protect the environment;
- express abilities and curiosity;
- explore and research alone, and with others (both peers and adults);
- reinforce a sense of autonomy and security;
- experience beauty, comfort, sensory stimulation, excitement, wonder, and joy.

To accomplish these outcomes, outdoor environments should feature (1) different types of play areas and designated play zones; (2) learning centers; and (3) transition areas. Outdoor environments should also allow for transformability and flexibility, include a variety of natural elements, and provide inviting opportunities for children to be actively engaged with nature (Ceppi and Zini 1998, National Arbor Day Foundation 2007). Many of the natural elements in the outdoor playspace should be in the form of loose parts that can be manipulated, changed, and moved about (e.g. stones, leaves, twigs, pine cones, etc). "Materials that can be moved, manipulated, and changed feed developmental needs" (Nicolson and Shipstead 2002: 352).

## Different types of play areas

A well-designed outdoor playspace will feature open areas for physically active play and protected quiet spaces for resting, watching, or engaging in less physically active pursuits. As outlined by Greenman (2005), outdoor environments for children should also provide places to be human, places for creative and constructive play, and places offering rich opportunities for environmental or nature play. Such environments, Greenman (1988) notes, "offer children education at its most compelling" (quoted in Elliot 2008: 4).

Places to be human should offer places of shelter; places to watch, to wonder, and to retreat; places to rest; places to eat; easy access to places to be diapered and to go to the bathroom; places to discover; and places that feel different (micro-climates that are sunny, shady, breezy, still, etc.). Places for creative and constructive play should provide children with opportunities for building, for using machines (wagons, digging tools, pulleys, etc.), for engaging in different forms of creative expression (painting, working with clay, etc.), and for pretending. Places for nature play should offer places to dig, watery places, places for growing, places for animal life, opportunities for collecting and carrying, and places for measuring (amount of rainfall, temperature, wind speed, length of shadows, etc.).

These different types of play areas can be overlapping, and all should include some natural elements. Trees and/or other types of plants should be incorporated into each of these areas. In choosing plants, care must be taken to avoid anything that may be poisonous or harmful to the children in other ways (e.g. sharp thorns).

## Designated zones

While different types of play areas should be offered, specific play zones should also be established. Five different play zones frequently cited in the literature (sometimes with different labels) are nature zone, adventure zone, active play zone, quiet play zone, and quiet retreat zone (Guddemi and Eriksen 1992, Wilson 2004). To encourage nature play, each of these areas should include a variety of natural elements.

A nature zone features such natural elements as trees, water, boulders, bushes, and other types of plants. It might also include mounds of earth for children to climb, a digging area where children are given the freedom to dig in the dirt, a sand pit, flower beds and vegetable plants, bird baths and bird feeders, a rain gauge, and a windsock. Ideally, a nature zone or natural area will also include a variety of wildlife (birds, butterflies, toads, snails, and earthworms). Weather permitting, this area may also include a pet rabbit or guinea pig. Creative play in a natural area often takes the form of role playing (e.g. pretending to be an animal, gardener, or explorer), making collages with natural materials (dried grasses, seeds, leaves, etc.), and experimenting with different materials (e.g. mixing water and sand, testing the "heaviness" of a bucket of stones, etc.).

The adventure zone is designed for more active play with rich opportunities for construction. It includes a variety of construction tools and materials. This need not include hammers and nails as building blocks, well-sanded pieces of lumber, old bicycle tires, vinyl gutters, stones, and wooden pallets work quite well. Creative play in this area includes the construction of ramps, bridges, pens, walls, and dens. Adding such natural materials as sticks, piles of leaves, twigs, and sand can greatly enrich the play value of this play zone and encourage children to make positive connections with nature. The children may, for example, decide to build dens and nests as well as roads and fences.

The active play zone provides for such activities as running, jumping, sliding, using wheeled toys, and playing ball (kicking, throwing, catching, bouncing, rolling). To accommodate such activities, the active play zone should include hard-surface areas as well as grass-covered or other soft-surface areas. Wheeled toys and bouncing balls work best on the hard-surface areas, while different types of "rough and tumble play" (such as jumping, running, wrestling, rolling) work best in a soft-surface area. Creative play in this area can take many different forms – from forming a "train" with wheeled toys to "becoming" wild ponies running up and down a hilly area.

The quiet play zone provides an alternative to active play. Some children are not as interested in "rough and tumble play" as others. They may enjoy less active dramatic play – such as playing house or working in an office, store, or veterinarian clinic. They may also enjoy painting outdoors, drawing with chalk on the sidewalk, and using clay to make a variety of shapes and figures. The quiet play zone should include a variety of art materials and dramatic play props. It should also include small tables or work benches. Large tree stumps or logs can also be used as work spaces. To encourage nature play in this area, add leaves, flower petals, and other natural materials for art-related activities; and include such dramatic play props as small gardening tools, straw hats, straw (loose straw and/or straw bales), flower pots, and pine cones.

A quiet retreat zone provides an additional alternative to active play. Establishing a quiet zone area in an outdoor playspace for young children is often overlooked and underrated (Wellhousen 2002). Some children tire easily – from physical activity and/or intense social interaction. For them, a quiet place to retreat is comforting and reassuring. They can feel safe and secure in having a special place with fewer physical and/or social demands. The quiet retreat zone should never be used for punishment or an imposed "time-out." It should always be self-chosen, and children's time there should be respected.

A quiet retreat zone can be used to meet the needs of individuals and the group. It can be used for reading, storytelling, eating lunch or snacks, holding class meetings, or just resting and watching. A quiet retreat zone should offer attractive niches and small benches. For infants and toddlers, this zone may consist of a blanket under a shady tree. The quiet zone may also include gazing balls, wind chimes, and windsocks. Attractive containers (e.g. baskets, wooden bowls, etc.) with a collection of natural and other unique materials (shells, pine cones, marbles, pebbles, seed pods, large buttons, etc.) add interest and invite individual or small group creative play activities.

While different play zones should have some type of boundary or demarcation, they should not be viewed as isolated units. Connections between them should be clearly visible and easily accessible. Children should be free to move their activities and materials from one play zone to another. They should be able to combine materials within and between the various zones. "Children can be thwarted in their play simply because they are not allowed to move something from one area to the next" (Bilton 2002: 49). Allowing them to combine materials encourages children to develop their own ideas and use their imaginations.

Boundaries between zones can consist of changes in ground covering or landscape elevation, or be formed by shrubs or other types of plants. One program for infants featured a grassy berm as a boundary between a quiet play area and a sand pit. Infants could crawl over the berm and experience the element of surprise or delight when they discovered the sand area which, to them, was out of sight as they played in the quiet area.

After years of research on the benefits of authentic play in intentionally designed natural spaces, the Dimensions Educational Research Foundation (National Arbor Day Foundation 2007) developed ten guiding principles for effective outdoor learning environments for young children. These principles (presented in Box 2.1) are consistent with the recommendations proposed elsewhere in this chapter, including the idea of having a mix of activity areas. Ten different areas are recommended (entry feature, open area for large-motor activities, climbing/crawling area, "messy" materials area, building area, nature art area, music and movement area, a garden and/ or pathway through plantings, a gathering area, and a storage area), with six additional "supplemental" areas (water area, dirt-digging area, sand area, wheeled-toy area, area for swings or other dynamic equipment, and a greenhouse.). Additional ideas proposed in these principles include assigning simple names to each area (e.g. action area, messy materials area, garden area, etc.) and marking each area with a sign and other visual clues as to its primary focus.

# Learning centers

In addition to play zones in the outdoor environment, a variety of learning centers or learning bays should also be provided. These are learning areas, each with a focused type of activity (e.g. art, dramatic play, block building, etc.). Wellhousen (2002) suggests exploring the learning centers found in preschool and kindergarten classrooms and then replicating these in the outdoor playspace with attention to supplies more

---

**Box 2.1** Ten guiding principles

1. Divide the space into clearly delineated areas for different kinds of activities.
2. Include a complete mix of activity areas.
3. Give areas simple names.
4. Identify each area with a sign and other visual clues.
5. Be sure every area is visible at all times.
6. Use a variety of natural materials, including trees and other live plants.
7. Choose elements for durability and low maintenance.
8. Maximize beauty and visual clarity in the overall design.
9. Personalize the design with regional materials and ideas from children and staff.
10. Be sure the space meets all regulatory standards for your region.

Source: National Arbor Day Foundation (2007), *Learning with Nature Idea Book*. Lincoln, NE: National Arbor Day Foundation.

suited for outdoor use. Typical learning centers include art, blocks, dramatic play, and books. Some of these centers can be arranged on wheeled carts, so that they can be transported easily back inside to protect the materials from the weather.

Perhaps the most important of these learning centers is the dramatic play area (Bilton 2002). Dramatic play invites creativity and social interaction in multiple ways. It also fosters an understanding of self and others and evokes critical development and learning skills – including the ability to work cooperatively, to negotiate, share, discuss, anticipate, and conclude. While the importance of the indoor dramatic play areas should not be overlooked, dramatic play outdoors provides "much more scope for movement and the play can be on a larger scale and involve the whole child" (Bilton 2002: 53).

Dramatic play needs to be available every day – its form, however, should change periodically. The form of dramatic play is influenced by the props and space provided. The outdoor dramatic play center can be housed under a shady tree, in a gazebo, on a platform, in the quiet play area, in the nature area, or in the adventure area. While props can be strategically placed in a specified area, children should be free to move them about at their discretion as long as they are not disrupting the play of other children. See Table 2.1 for a listing of different learning centers that might be used outdoors and examples of materials that could be included.

Incorporating learning centers in the outdoor setting offers multiple advantages: it "gives children more choices, extends the time they will spend in a play area, and contributes to the overall appropriateness of outdoor play" (Wellhousen 2002: 81). Additionally, arranging a play/learning environment around learning centers helps to ensure that a balance of activities and learning opportunities is available.

Some learning centers may be incorporated into one of the play zones on an ongoing basis – art in the quiet play area, for example. Others may be housed temporarily in one play zone and then moved to another at a later time. For example, a dramatic play area may be set up in the nature zone as a "camping experience" at one time and set up in the adventure area as a "repair shop" at another time.

One concern relating to learning centers outdoors is the upkeep and housing of equipment and materials. In many programs, the materials used for outdoor learning centers have to be put away at the end of the day. This is not only time consuming and disruptive to the flow of activities, it can also be frustrating to children who want to "pick up where they left off" the day before.

In one instance, a small group of children had constructed a bus transportation system in the adventure area with roads, bus stops, and posted schedules. A wagon tied to a tricycle became the bus. Bus passes were carefully drawn, and a box (a cardboard envelope box) to collect fares was attached to the handlebars of the tricycle. Soon after the children had created these dramatic play components, it was time for them to go inside and get ready for dismissal. The wheeled equipment had to be moved into a storage shed; the signs and bus passes protected from the weather; and the paper, cardboard, markers, and pencils brought inside.

When the children went outside the next day, there was no sign of the bus transportation system that had been in place. One child asked another, "Wanna play bus again?" The child's response was "No, I don't want to." If the bus scene had remained in place or was easy to assemble, the response might have been entirely different.

**Table 2.1**  Outdoor learning centers

| Center | Materials |
| --- | --- |
| Art center | Work tables and easels |
| | Art supplies (paper, crayons, scissors, glue, clay, tape, etc.) |
| Manipulative center | Work table |
| | Work trays |
| | Containers for items (baskets, boxes, egg cartons, etc.) |
| | Puzzles |
| | Pattern blocks |
| | Small objects (buttons, marbles, natural materials, etc.) |
| | Science materials (measuring cups, hand lens, etc.) |
| Block/ building center | Large hollow blocks |
| | Milk crates |
| | Cardboard boxes |
| | Planks |
| | Ladders |
| | Plastic tubing |
| | Hose pipe |
| | Buckets |
| | Stones and other natural materials (twigs, bark, shells, etc.) |
| | Large pieces of fabric |
| Dramatic play center | Platform or other specified area |
| | Places to sit (logs, stumps, benches, blanket, etc.) |
| | Materials/props to motivate role playing: |
| | • dress-up clothes |
| | • dolls |
| | • stuffed animals |
| | • large appliance boxes |
| | • dishes and other household items |
| | • yard and gardening supplies (wheelbarrows, rakes, etc.) |
| | • camping equipment |
| | • backpacks. |
| Book/library center | Reading materials (books, maps, brochures, etc.) |
| | Writing materials |
| | Picture cards |
| | Places to sit |
| | Place to write |

Some visible evidence of what had occurred the day before may have motivated the children to continue with the bus activity. Once continued, it may have evolved to another level of thinking and interacting.

It's important to find ways to provide continuity of play experiences over time. Children should be able to continue the play they started one day without having to start all over again the next day. They need time to develop a theme and explore different materials and potential layouts. A one-day set up limits their opportunities to use materials in different ways and to modify their activities. Motivation and concentration increase as children are able to follow an interest over a period of time (Bilton 2002).

To minimize disruption to an activity, clean up and storage at the end of the day should be as smooth as possible. A shed or other type of protected storage for movable equipment (bikes, wagons, balls, shovels, buckets, etc.) is critical. This shed or storage area should be large enough to store materials in an orderly and easily accessible way. Lines marking off parking spaces for wheeled equipment help prevent stacking and shoving. Shelves, hooks, and durable storage boxes and baskets add a sense of order. A wheeled cart with shelves makes it easy to move materials as needed. One program used an old library cart for this.

Some documentation of what occurred during a play episode can also bridge the gap between one day and the next. This documentation can be in the form of photos, sketches, and/or written text. Involving children in the documentation can be motivating and instructive. In addition to recording some of the play activities and discoveries made in the process of one play episode, the documentation could also include some ideas offered by the children as to what they plan to do in that play area the next day. For example, "When we play 'bus' tomorrow, I have to stop at the gas station. I need gas and want the windows washed."

## Transition areas

Transition areas are also important in the layout of an outdoor playspace. When designed appropriately, transition areas improve the flow of people from one area to another. Ideally, movement between spaces is experienced as physically and emotionally smooth: "The more abrupt the transition, the more difficult the experience" (Greenman 2005: 77).

A well-constructed pathway represents one type of transition area that helps children move from one area to another. "Without clear pathways, circulation creates confusion, anxiety, aggression, and congestion" (Greenman 2005: 79). Pathways should be engaging in themselves. They should offer different motor experiences. This can be accomplished through variety in surfaces and grades, or through the addition of steps and railings. To add interest, stepping stones, tunnels, planks, benches, and flower pots can be incorporated into the design of a pathway. Mosaic stepping stones can be made with the help of the children.

Courtyards and foyers represent other types of transition areas. Windows and overhangs can also be used to help make the connection and ease the transition between an indoor and outdoor environment.

## Transformability and flexibility

The outdoor environment should encourage manipulation and transformation. Adults and children should be able to rearrange and recreate different aspects of the environment. This transformability and flexibility invites creativity and problem-solving. Loose parts play a critical role in the redesign of an outdoor playspace.

Loose parts are materials that children can manipulate and move about on their own. They can range from simple natural materials, such as pieces of bark, small stones, and seeds, to actual construction materials such as pieces of lumber, wire or plastic mesh, and strips of leather or "fat ropes." Traditional playgrounds rarely feature loose parts, as they tend to be messy – hard to keep clean and organized in the outdoor environment. But without loose parts, creative play is severely stymied.

Loose parts are critical to the success of play zones and learning centers – this is true for both indoor and outdoor settings. Loose parts add both complexity and variety to play units. A play unit is a single, designated area containing objects for play. A play unit may or may not have tangible boundaries. Play units with tangible boundaries include a bicycle path, a sandbox, and a water table. The area around a five-foot (1.52m) section of a log is an example of a play unit without a tangible boundary. Complexity refers to a certain quality of a play unit – that is the extent to which children can actively manipulate or alter the play potential of the unit.

There are three different levels of complexity often used to critique play units: simple, complex, and super. A simple play unit has one obvious use, and there are no available loose parts or accessories. Most equipment on traditional playgrounds (swings, slides, climbing structures) represent simple play units. Such units offer little potential for creative play. A complex play unit includes two different types of play materials, allowing some manipulation by the children. A sandbox with plastic cups is an example of a complex play unit. Children can fill and empty the cups. They can pour sand from one cup to another, or they can scoop the sand up with their hands to fill the cups. The complex play unit allows children some degree of improvisation. Adding one or more additional play materials to a complex unit transforms it into a super play unit. Funnels and sieves added to the sandbox with plastic cups, for example, transform the play unit from a complex to a super level of complexity. Increasing complexity (from simple, to complex, to super) enhances the potential for creative play. It also extends the time children remain interested in a play unit (Wellhousen 2002).

Dramatic play and physical exploration usually do not flourish on equipment-only playgrounds, as such environments tend to divert children to gross motor activities and fail to provide the necessary materials to stimulate dramatic or constructive play. Activities in equipment-only playgrounds do not spiral upwards in complexity. The play value and learning potential are thus seriously limited.

Variety is another factor that enhances the potential of a play unit. Variety in play units relates to the types of experiences children can have while engaged in related play activities. The cups in the sandbox, for example, allow children to fill and pour. Adding more containers – such as plastic bottles and small buckets – while increasing the number of materials, doesn't provide a greater variety of experiences. Children would still be filling and pouring. Adding funnels and sieves, on the other hand, increases the variety of experiences. Adding a spray bottle filled with water would enhance the variety even more.

In choosing loose parts, both complexity and variety should be considered. For fostering creative play, natural items (sticks, leaves, rocks, seeds, grasses, flowers, pods, shells, moss, etc.) are ideal. Their potential for adding complexity and variety with natural materials is almost endless.

## Sense of place

An additional consideration when planning an outdoor playspace for young children is how it helps children develop a "sense of place." The term "place," when used in this context, doesn't mean simply a geographic location. Rather, place in this context refers to location plus other factors that give that location its unique character. Such factors in children's environments often include opportunities for seclusion (as in "secret" dens or other nest-like refuges), exploration, and manipulation. Complexity, diversity, opportunities for immersion or direct encounters with the natural world, and opportunities for experiencing "magical moments" can also contribute to a "sense of place" experience.

One benefit of sense-of-place experiences is the way they foster attachment to a particular place and the unique elements of that place. If those places are natural places, children's affinity for the natural world is likely to deepen. Another benefit of sense-of-place experiences is the positive effect it can have on a child's developing sense of self (Elliot 2008). A warm, nurturing, stimulating environment tells children

**Photograph 2.1**  Tunnel in children's garden

29

that they are competent and valued and that their way of learning is understood and respected. A dull, disorganized, or impoverished environment, on the other hand, may give children the message that they are not valued, competent, or respected. Such messages impact strongly on how children perceive themselves as learners and explorers.

Sense-of-place experiences can also affect children's attitudes and values towards the world of nature and their role as caretakers or guardians of the land (Elliot 2008, Nabhan and Trimble 1994). Learning to love and care for one particular place can lead to a lifelong commitment to care for a wider world of natural places.

For most young children, the first public place they come to know intimately is their preschool or primary school. Required inspections of the school building and grounds usually focus almost exclusively on safety issues. It would be well, however, if other aspects of the environment would also be considered, especially in relation to the quality of the outdoor environment. Fortunately, there are a number of organizations dedicated to working with schools to help them transform their outdoor spaces into positive learning habitats for children by adding or enhancing opportunities for direct interactions with the natural world. Such organizations include the Royal Society for the Protection of Birds (RSPB), Learning Through Landscapes, the National Wildlife Federation, Dimensions Educational Research Foundation, and the Natural Learning Initiative. See Appendix 2 for a brief description of each of these organizations.

In addition to preserving or creating natural areas around the school where children can immerse themselves in nature, a sense of place can also be fostered by giving children the opportunity to personalize spaces and places to make some aspects of the environment uniquely theirs. School environments, in too many cases, tend to be institutional in nature. It's difficult for children in such environments to feel that the place "belongs" to them. Encouraging children to create, change, and personalize spaces and places can counteract some of the otherwise generic elements of the school environment and foster feelings of attachment. A variety of loose parts – including natural materials and other art- and construction-related materials – will invite children to create a place that reflects their interests and capabilities.

Adults can organize additional activities around the idea of personalizing a place. One preschool program did this by creating an "alphabet garden" where individual pots of plants corresponded to children's names. First name initials were used for determining the correspondence: peas for Pam, carrots for Cindi, strawberries for Stan, etc. Personalizing a place and helping children feel "ownership" of a place can also be accomplished by involving children in the ongoing development and care of the yard. Ways to do this include having children help with mulching and watering plants, maintaining bird baths and bird feeders, composting, raking, etc.

Finding ways to certify a place can also foster attachment to a place. Certification in this context means spotlighting a particular place and presenting it in some way to the public. One school did this by using a drawing of their gardens as the illustration on their holiday greeting cards. Another school completed the process of being certified as a "wildlife habitat" through the National Wildlife Federation and then inviting the local newspaper and TV station to publicize their work.

## Guidelines and checklists

Guidelines for excellence in early childhood education and environmental education indicate that children should have daily opportunities for outdoor play in stimulating environments (Copple and Bredekamp 2009, NAAEE 2010). As articulated by the National Association for the Education of Young Children (NAEYC), outdoor playspaces should be designed to foster the development of gross motor skills, provide opportunities for children to play freely and loudly, and help children learn about the natural environment (Bredekamp and Copple 1997). While many playgrounds meet the first two of these design considerations (i.e. fostering motor development and allowing children to play freely and loudly), opportunities to learn about the natural environment are often overlooked. Such an oversight represents a missed opportunity for fostering holistic development and promoting positive, caring relationships with the natural world.

Opportunities for children to learn about the natural environment can be maximized by developing natural playspaces for young children. To get started, the criteria presented in Box 2.2 might be helpful. Adherence to these criteria will reap benefits for both children and the environment.

Some checklists for outdoor play areas focus almost exclusively on maintenance and other safety concerns. Following are some typical items found on such checklists:

- Outdoor play area is free of miscellaneous debris, litter, or animal feces.
- There is no standing water.
- The area is appropriately enclosed.
- Protective surfacing material is appropriate.
- All zones are free of tripping hazards.
- All equipment is free of protrusions and projections such as nuts, bolts, or bar ends.

While such safety-related considerations are critical when evaluating an outdoor playspace, they should be viewed as only one part of an overall evaluation. Other items should focus on comfort, beauty, opportunities for sensory stimulation, accessibility, flexibility, physical, social, and mental challenges, as well as rich opportunities for hands-on interaction with nature. Presented in Box 2.3 is a checklist that includes some of these ideas.

## Creating an environmental yard – one program's story

Some people may find that reading about and/or visiting elaborate playgardens is inspiring but intimidating. They may think their level of expertise and budget constraints would keep them from ever doing anything like that. But everyone can develop an environmental yard – even if all that they have to work with is a flower pot, soil, and a handful of seeds.

One program, working with a budget of less than $500, added over twenty nature-related elements to their outdoor playspace to create an environmental yard (Wilson *et al.* 1996). Many of the additions were designed to help children learn about animals

**Box 2.2**  Criteria for planning and developing a natural playspace for young children

1.  Demonstrate respect for the natural environment:
    - Avoid unnecessary destruction of the natural environment.
    - Take proper care of living things.
    - Recycle or reuse materials for new constructions and additional play equipment.
    - Avoid toxic chemicals.
    - Include a variety of native plants. (Native plants are hardier than imported plants and provide food and shelter for local wildlife.)
2.  Provide opportunities for direct involvement:
    - Provide a wide variety of "loose parts."
    - Provide opportunities for sensory-rich experiences.
    - Make accommodations for children with special needs.
3.  Attend to safety and comfort:
    - Provide adequate protection from the elements (wind, rain, sun, etc.).
    - Provide areas for rest.
    - Use soft ground covers in areas where children run, jump, and climb.
    - Avoid poisonous plants and other toxic materials.
    - Provide "sheltering" areas.
    - Ensure open vision lines for proper adult supervision.
    - Separate areas for infants and toddlers from areas for older children.
4.  Include elements that foster appreciation and understanding of the natural environment:
    - Develop a variety of gardens.
    - Include a variety of bushes, trees, and other types of vegetation.
    - Provide places and materials that invite wildlife.
    - Provide materials that draw attention to environmental changes (rain gauge, windsock, etc.).
    - Select plants that change with the seasons.
5.  Include elements that relate to children's interest and enjoyment and that stimulate the senses:
    - Provide opportunities for a wide variety of activities that relate to diverse interests and abilities.
    - Design areas and provide materials that invite social interaction.
    - Design plant settings that define enclosures for children.
    - Include a variety of topographical features and ground covers.
    - Provide opportunities for healthy risk taking. (Balance risk with safety. Know the difference between a risk and a hazard: a risk is possible to negotiate; a hazard is inherently dangerous (Curtis 2010).)
    - Provide a variety of dramatic play materials and settings.
    - Vary the form, size, texture, and shape of plants. (Some plants should be child size, others much larger. Some plants should have low hanging branches that children can touch. Branches on other plants should be

**Box 2.2**  continued

> much higher, forming a canopy and making interesting "sun and shadow" patterns on the ground.)
> - Select some plants for fragrance, some for taste, and some for sound (e.g. wind blowing through dry leaves).
> - Select plants that produce loose parts and "play props" (leaves, flowers, fruits, nuts, seeds, sticks, etc.).
> - Design plant settings and other outdoor features (fences, gates, walls, paths, etc.) that facilitate movement through the play areas.

6. Involve the community:
   - Invite community agency involvement.
   - Utilize outdoor skills and interest of parents and other community members.
7. Minimize the need for labor-intensive maintenance:
   - Keep or develop natural areas.
   - Use construction materials of high quality and appropriate for the local climate.

**Box 2.3**  Checklist for evaluating an outdoor playspace for young children
1. The environment is safe:
   - free of toxins
   - free of allergenic, poisonous, and spiky varieties of plants
   - provides fall-absorbing surfaces in all equipment settings
   - free of steep slopes and sudden drop-offs
   - well-maintained equipment
   - well-supervised
   - hard-surface paths separated from other play areas
   - play area securely separated from traffic
   - provides hand rails and non-skid surfaces where needed
   - is properly drained
   - has clearly-defined boundaries between play settings
   - no visual barriers for supervision
   - adequate space around swings and climbing equipment.
2. The environment is comfortable:
   - provides shade
   - features sunny areas
   - protects from cold wind
   - includes places to sit (for children and adults)
   - provides access to fresh drinking water
   - includes small spaces for quiet play (by one to five children)
   - includes a variety of well-defined zones to accommodate different groups of children and different activities

**Box 2.3** continued

      • includes transition areas between buildings and outdoors (e.g. terraces, decks, patios, etc.).

3. The environment is interesting and inviting:
   • dominated by natural elements (plants, stones, soil, sand, etc.)
   • includes a variety of surfaces and terrains
   • attracts wildlife
   • offers a variety of social spaces (for different size groups and different types of activities).

4. The environment is stimulating:
   • features different colors, scents, textures, and sounds
   • provides for a variety of activities
   • offers high places from which to view the area
   • offers different-sized spaces to crawl in, under, over, or through
   • invites interaction with the natural environment.

5. The environment is flexible:
   • includes "loose parts" that can be manipulated and moved about
   • includes undefined spaces and objects which children can use for creative and fantasy play
   • invites open-ended interaction and exploration.

6. The environment is accessible:
   • includes child-sized tables and benches
   • offers several skill levels or levels of difficulty (e.g. high, higher, highest)
   • includes wheelchair accessible entrances, ramps, paths, tables, playground equipment, etc.
   • accessible at all times and in all kinds of weather.

7. The environment is challenging:
   • provides opportunities for healthy risk taking for children with varying abilities.

8. The environment promotes a sense of wonder:
   • aesthetically pleasing
   • includes materials which draw attention to sensory-rich aspects of the environment (e.g. wind chimes, windsocks, water drums, gazing globes, etc.).

9. The environment reflects the local landscape and climate:
   • features native plants
   • includes natural habitats for native animals
   • includes elements or features that call attention to the local weather and climate.

10. The environment promotes a sense of place:
    • includes unique features that appeal to young children
    • includes features that personalize the space for children.

Adapted from Wilson (2004: 20)

and animal habitats. What they added included a bird bath, bird house, bird feeder, herb garden, outdoor thermometer, binoculars, cold frame, compost pile, seedlings for bushes, windsock, wind chimes, animal costumes, animal puppets, movable cart with books and art materials, painting easel, and an assortment of loose parts (mostly natural materials – shells, pine cones, stones, etc.). The bird bath was made by turning a large plastic flower pot upside down and placing a saucer on top of it. A small rock was used to help hold the saucer in place and allow the birds a place to land.

One type of animal habitat (for pretend play) was introduced by creating two large wooden boxes (two by two and a half feet (0.6m × 0.76m)) with two solid sides, two rung sides, and two open sides. A lumber yard donated the wood and the labor in making these boxes. Children use the boxes as dens and hiding places. The boxes are also used as supports for boards and ladders. Because the boxes aren't too heavy or too large for the children to move about (especially when the children work in pairs), they provide an excellent way for the children to manipulate their own environment. Animal costumes were added to foster role playing. These were handmade and donated by a parent of one of the children in the program. Once she heard about the environmental yard project, she was eager to contribute.

Fast-growing bushes were planted in a corner of the yard to attract birds. The bird bath and bird feeder were also put in this area. Other gardening activities included converting a child's broken shopping cart into a movable flower garden. A herb garden was planted inside a large discarded tractor tire. Children got involved in this activity by filling their wagon and wheelbarrow with dirt, building a ramp up onto the tire with a large wooden block and plank, dumping the dirt in the middle of the tire, and finally planting the herbs.

Pea seeds were planted in handfuls of soil placed in sandwich bags. The bags were taped to the window inside, so that the children could easily watch the roots grow down and the stems shoot up. When ready, the peas were transplanted outside under a simple cold frame. The cold frame was made from two bales of straw pushed up against the building and a wooden window frame covered in clear plastic.

Pre- and post-discussions with the children indicated increased interest in and understanding of the natural world. Teacher feedback suggested the children also developed language, mathematical, and problem-solving skills through this project (Wilson *et al.* 1996).

# Bringing the outdoors in

All education is environmental education.

(David Orr)

Creative play and learning through nature can occur indoors as well as outdoors, but this requires bringing elements of nature inside. There are many ways to do this. Natural materials can be added to the physical environment. Nature can be used as a central theme for planned activities, and nature-related posters, books, and manipulatives (puzzles, toy figurines, etc.) can be used to draw attention to the world of nature. Nature can, in fact, be used as an integrating context for all classroom displays, activities and experiences. This involves using nature-related themes and concepts in all areas of teaching and learning.

The idea of using the environment as an integrating context (EIC) for learning is not new. The EIC model was first developed and field tested by the State Education and Environment Roundtable (SEER) under the leadership of Dr Gerald Lieberman in the 1990s. Related research findings indicate that students learn more effectively within an environment-based context than within a traditional educational framework. When the EIC model was used, students performed better in mathematics, science, social studies, and language arts than their peers in traditional programs (Lieberman and Hooty 1998). Findings also indicated that students in the EIC programs had fewer discipline problems, and students at risk of academic failure worked better and learned more effectively (Grant 1998).

The EIC model has since been used in the development of curriculum for grades kindergarten through high school for the state of California. This curriculum – referred to as the EEI (Education and Environment Initiative) curriculum – consists of eighty-five units addressing select science and history–social science academic standards. Something similar is occurring in some early childhood settings. Nature preschools are an example of this.

A nature preschool is a preschool – or early childhood program – with a nature focus. Children in a nature preschool spend some time outdoors every day, interacting with the natural environment. Nature preschools offer indoor activities, as well, but incorporate nature themes and materials throughout the activities. Most nature preschools do not emphasize "academic learning" but focus instead on development of the whole child and positive connections with nature (Finch 2005). More descriptive information about one specific nature preschool – the Schlitz Audubon Nature Preschool – is presented in Appendix 1.

## The physical environment

The overall effect of the physical environment in an early childhood setting should not be left to chance, as it plays a critical role in fostering children's learning and impacting their emotions (Duncan 2011). In some traditions, the environment is considered to be the "third teacher," with parents and teachers as the other two. The Reggio Emilia approach is a prime example of this. Reggio Emilia classrooms are generally filled with plants and natural light. Large windows look out into courtyards, and attempts are made to integrate each of the classrooms with the rest of the school and the surrounding community, with special attention to aesthetics and the natural environment.

The Reggio philosophy includes the idea that one of the benefits of beauty is that it helps children focus or concentrate (Klein 2011). Others, too, have suggested strong connections between beauty, nature, wonder, and knowledge (Deviney et al. 2010a, Deviney et al. 2010b, Montessori 1972).

Deviney and her co-authors (2010a, 2010b) suggest the following seven principles of design to enhance the aesthetic qualities of the indoor environment of an early childhood classroom. Each of these principles addresses nature directly or invites the incorporation of nature-related elements.

1. Nature inspires beauty.
2. Color generates interest.
3. Furnishings define space.
4. Texture adds depth.
5. Displays enhance environment.
6. Elements heighten ambiance.
7. Focal points attract attention.

Bringing natural materials into the physical environment of the classroom is one way to foster learning about and appreciation of the natural environment. As learning centers are a common feature in many early childhood programs, adding natural elements to these centers is one avenue for bringing the outdoors in. Presented in Table 3.1 are some ideas for making natural materials and other nature-related materials a part of different learning centers. The natural materials invite a variety of nature play activities, while the nature-related materials can foster additional understandings about nature and/or the theme of the center.

Another way to bring the outdoors in is to set up different nature-themed environments. You might convert the entire classroom into a woods or beach, for

**Table 3.1** Natural and nature-related materials in learning centers

| Learning center | Natural and nature-related materials |
| --- | --- |
| Language/literacy | Animal puppets, nature-related flannel board cut-outs, books about nature, nature-related pictures, nature-related writing prompts (e.g. I like trees. They are ...) |
| Blocks | Pebbles, sticks, twigs, pine cones |
| Texture table | Pine cones, shells, leaves, sand, pebbles, grass, corn cobs, corn husk, corn silk, wheat stalks, soil and mud, twigs and sand paper, spray bottle with water |
| Art | Shells, seeds, leaves, dried grass, corn cobs, dried wheat stalks, clay, flower petals and leaves |
| Music | Natural materials for making shakers (e.g. kernels of corn or wheat and small boxes or plastic bottles), sticks for drumming, CDs with sounds of nature (water falling, wind in the trees, birds singing, etc.) |
| Dramatic play | Camping equipment, child-sized gardening tools, explorer packs (with magnifying glasses, note pads and pencils, clipboards, binoculars, etc.), stuffed animals and puppets, park ranger hats and badges |
| Science | Aquarium, terrarium, abandoned bird's nest, snake skin, leaves, observation tools (magnifying glass) |
| Mathematics | Variety of natural objects (stones, seeds, feathers, etc.) for sorting, weighing, and measuring, sorting trays (e.g. egg cartons), measuring tools (scale, rulers, etc.) |

example, or just use one part of the room for a nature-themed environment. Don't overlook the value of mini-environments – a bird's nest or a fox's den, for example. You can make giant-sized versions of these mini-environments to accommodate children's play. Whenever possible, involve the children in making the nature-themed environments and use as many natural materials as possible.

## Live plants and animals

Live plants and animals should also be a part of the indoor environment. While some plants may be more permanent parts of the environment and serve primarily a decorative role, others may be in the room for only a short while – cut flowers, for example – and observed more closely for change over time. Whenever possible, involve children in the care of plants – watering a potted plant, opening a shade to provide more light for a plant, adding wilted flowers to a compost pile, etc. Also involve children in growing plants from seeds and bulbs. Grow some plants that can be transplanted outdoors, especially plants that produce food (peas, corn, etc.). A hint for involving children in watering plants is to have them use a spray bottle versus a watering can or bucket. With a spray bottle, children are less likely to overwater the plants.

Following are a few additional ideas for adding plants to the indoor environment:

- Promote the environmentally friendly practice of reusing by making a "junk garden." Use such "junk items" as an old kettle, worn-out boot, or empty milk carton for container gardening.
- Grow a sweet potato vine in a glass jar. A wonderful thing about sweet potatoes is that they aren't just good to eat: they also make an interesting houseplant. A sweet potato vine grows quickly and can thrive in a jar of water. This makes it an excellent plant to grow with children. They can see the vine and the roots change over time. Choose a sweet potato that is firm and if possible one that already has buds or "eyes." Either the red or yellow variety works well. Insert toothpicks into the potato on all four sides at the center of the potato. Place the potato in a jar of water. The toothpicks will keep the potato upright in the jar. Set the jar where it will get lots of sunshine. Shoots will begin to appear within a few days and roots within a week or so.

Live animals are a little more complex for keeping indoors, but the outcomes can be fun and rewarding. The opportunity to observe animals at close range sets the stage for many interesting and stimulating learning experiences. Children are fascinated by animals and, if given the opportunity, will spend considerable time observing the characteristics and behaviors of animals. They'll ask questions, ask to be involved in the care and feeding of the animal, and become emotionally attached to an animal that becomes familiar to them.

In addition to learning about the animal and what it needs to survive, children involved in the care of a classroom pet will also develop a sense of stewardship and responsibility towards other living things. As children realize that the animal is a living thing just as they are living, they will be ready to take the perspective of the animal in relation to what it needs to thrive – food, shelter, protection from harm, etc. Perspective-taking is a critical step in their social, emotional, and ecological development (Harlan 1992).

Tending to the needs of animals requires children to give thought and attention to something outside themselves and supports the practice of caring. Some research supports the idea that as children care for animals, they become more caring towards people as well (Rud and Beck 2000).

A number of different animals can be kept successfully in an early childhood setting and provide the children with valuable learning experiences. There are, however, a number of issues to be considered to ensure the success of the experience. Planning is the first and one of the most important steps in the process. Following are some questions that will need to be addressed:

- What type of animal should be selected?
- What are the animal's habitat needs, and how can these needs be met in the classroom?
- What's involved in the care of the animal – what does it eat, when does it sleep, how will it get exercise, what frightens the animal or makes it uncomfortable, etc.?
- Is it safe for the children to handle the animal?
- What will I do with the animal during program breaks (during holidays, etc.)?

39

■   Are there any legal considerations related to the confinement of the animal – such as what animals can be collected from the wild, how long can they be confined, how should they be returned to the wild, etc.?

The first and probably the most important decision to make about introducing an animal into an early childhood setting is selecting the type of animal to have. Will it be an animal collected from the wild and kept on a temporary basis, or will it be a classroom pet, such as a cat, dog, guinea pig, or rabbit? Factors to be considered in making this decision should include the health and safety of the children and the health and daily care of the animal. Children should never be at risk, and animals should always receive appropriate respect and care. Be sure to check with parents for any possible allergy-related concerns.

Presented below are some additional guidelines for selecting animals for an early childhood setting. These guidelines are based, in part, on the work of David Kramer (1992) and professional organizations in the fields of education and veterinary medicine.

■   Smaller animals are generally better than larger animals.
■   Native animals are generally better than exotic ones.
■   Wild mammals, venomous animals, and sick or injured animals should never be kept in the classroom.
■   No animal should be kept in the classroom unless:
    –   it is hardy and can thrive in captivity;
    –   its natural habitat can be duplicated indoors;
    –   its normal behavior can be expressed in the enclosure;
    –   it can adjust to the classroom conditions (temperature, lighting, noise level, etc.);
    –   it can be properly cared for at all times by someone knowledgeable about its needs.

After selecting a type of animal for the classroom, the next step is acquiring that animal. If not in conflict with local regulations, some animals can be collected from a nearby natural habitat (e.g. earthworms, spiders, tadpoles, insects, etc.). Others can be purchased from a reputable pet store or dealer.

Once an animal is introduced into the classroom, children should be given instructions on how to handle the animal in a safe and respectful way. Adults should always monitor children as they handle an animal and make sure that children wash their hands immediately before and after handling animals.

A few books may be helpful when adding an animal to the classroom environment. While not a recent publication, *Snail Trails, and Tadpole Tails* by Cohen and Tunick (1997) is an excellent resource for creating mini-habitats in the classroom for five different animals: worms, snails, tadpoles, silkworms, and praying mantises. *The Salamander Room* by Ann Mazer (1994) is a beautiful children's book that can be shared with the children as soon as an animal is introduced into the classroom or discussion about getting such an animal comes up. *The Salamander Room* is a story about a young boy who finds a salamander and wants to keep it in his room. His mother asks a series of questions to draw attention to what the salamander will need to live inside the house.

How long an animal should remain inside the classroom depends to a large extent on the type of animal involved and the purpose for keeping the animal. Animals taken from their natural habitats should be chosen very carefully and never be kept for more than a week or so. After this time, they should be returned to where they were found. Involving children in this process can teach them valuable lessons about how to relate to the natural world in a caring and responsible way.

## Pro-nature books

Books and stories play an important role in most early childhood programs, and being able to select quality, age-appropriate literature is one of the expectations placed on early childhood educators. To help children learn about nature and develop positive attitudes about the natural world, teachers of young children should be familiar with "pro-nature books" and stories and share them with children in the classroom. Teachers of young children should also be familiar with the concept of using books and stories to guide children's thoughts and actions in pro-social ways. While doing this, however, teachers should keep in mind the importance of interactive discussion and the understanding that children construct their own meaning of the world around them. Books can serve as effective stimuli for meaningful discussion, but they don't "give" children attitudes and values. Rather than just reading a book from start to finish, teachers should help children "uncover" the meaning and personal implications of the story through thoughtful discussion. Keep in mind, however, that ideas relating to respect and empathy and understanding of what is right and wrong arises out of social interactions and social relationships (Coles 1997) – not out of explaining or telling.

A pro-nature book helps children develop accurate understandings and positive attitudes relating to the natural environment. Several factors to look for in identifying pro-nature books include (a) how the human/environment relationship is portrayed; (b) how nature and specific natural elements are portrayed; and (c) how caring for the environment is encouraged.

## How the human/environment relationship is portrayed

Some books may suggest that humans are somehow "separate from" versus "a part of" the rest of the natural world. Such books may present the natural environment as no more than a resource to be used by humans. While we want children to learn that everything we use comes ultimately from the natural world, it is not ecologically appropriate to suggest that we can relate to the natural environment as simply something that can be used. Aldo Leopold (1986) explains this concept in his articulation of the land ethic:

> The land ethic simply enlarges the boundaries of the community to include soils, waters, plants, and animals, or collectively: the land. … A land ethic changes the role of Homo sapiens from conqueror of the land-community to plain member and citizen of it.

41

The *Earth Charter*, too, addresses the need for humans to stand in "right relationship" with the land by respecting the intrinsic value of all of nature. As articulated in Principle I of the *Charter* ("Respect and Care for the Community of Life"), humans have an ethical responsibility to "recognize that all beings are interdependent and every form of life has value regardless of its worth to human beings."

*Make Way for Ducklings* by Robert McCloskey (1941) is a story that addresses the human/environment relationship in an ecologically appropriate way. The focus of the story is on the safety and welfare of the ducks and how people respond to help them. In one part of the story, traffic is stopped by a policeman to allow the ducks and their ducklings to cross the street safely. While making way for ducklings isn't a part of the policeman's job, his actions and the people's positive response represent a willingness to be slightly inconvenienced for the sake of the ducks. Such a willingness gives us some small indication of what is meant by being in "right relationship" with other living things.

## How nature and specific elements of nature are portrayed

Almost everyone knows a story or two about the "big bad wolf." In the story of "The Three Little Pigs," a wolf threatens to "huff and puff and blow their houses down." In the story of "Little Red Riding Hood," the wolf is also presented as an evil, mean creature ready to eat both the little girl and her grandmother. Such portrayals of the wolf can create false understandings and prejudices about nature in the minds of children.

Pro-nature books do the opposite – that is, they help children develop accurate understandings of the natural world and positive feelings towards nature. *Wonderful Worms* by Linda Glaser (1994) is an example of a non-fiction pro-nature book that portrays nature and specific natural elements in a positive way. Using simple text and full-color illustrations, *Wonderful Worms* explains the vital role earthworms play in an ecosystem.

## How caring for the environment is encouraged

Books and stories for children often carry hidden messages which can influence the way children think and act. A pro-nature book will suggest that they should relate to the environment in a caring way. The message need not be expressed explicitly, as in "We have to save the Earth." A far better approach is to introduce a likeable character (human or animal) who demonstrates what it means to care. *If You Were My Baby* by Fran Hodgkins (2007) is an example. This book focuses on the love and caring of mothers towards their offspring. The story includes a baby bat being held in its mother's protective embrace and a baby mountain goat being guided by its mother up high cliffs.

Caring for the environment can also be encouraged through a story or book about a particular natural place or specific natural element. While some may think of a desert as a dry, harsh place where no one would want to live, a picture book by Byrd Baylor (author) and Peter Parnall (illustrator) (1987) presents an entirely different picture. In *The Desert is Theirs,* children learn about the desert as a special place greatly loved by the people – and the animals – who "share the feeling of being brothers in the desert."

# Identifying pro-nature books

In addition to considering the three factors discussed above (i.e. how the human/environment relationship is portrayed, how nature and specific natural elements are portrayed, and how caring for the environment is encouraged), the following questions might also be helpful in identifying pro-nature books:

1. Do the characters in the story demonstrate an appreciation for nature and/or a sense of wonder about the natural world?
2. Do the characters show empathy and compassion for nature versus trying to dominate or control the natural world?

Presented in Table 3.2 are additional examples of pro-nature books.

**Table 3.2**  Examples of pro-nature books

| Title/author(s) | Pro-nature themes/characteristics |
| --- | --- |
| *Thanks to the Animals*, Sockabasin | Caring, positive attitudes about forest animals |
| *In My Backyard*, Ruurs | Positive portrayal of backyard animals |
| *The Very Best Bed*, Raye | Likeable animal character seeking a place to sleep |
| *Bear-ly There*, Raye | Demonstrates caring for a bear |
| *In a Nutshell*, Anthony and Arbo | Appreciation for the cycle of life |
| *Where Would I Be in an Evergreen Tree?* Blomberg and Gabriel | Positive portrayal of an evergreen tree and the life it supports |
| *Verdi*, Cannon | Positive portrayal of reptiles |
| *The Seaside Switch*, Kudklinski | Positive portrayal of the water's edge |
| *Blueberries for Sal*, McCloskey | Demonstrates mothers (including a bear) caring for their young |
| *The Carrot Seed*, Krauss | Understanding of how plants grow |
| *The Very Hungry Caterpillar*, Carle | Positive portrayal of a caterpillar; understanding of the life cycle of a butterfly |

## Minimizing walls

The title of this chapter, "Bringing the outdoors in," calls attention to the fact that we live in a society where "indoors" and "outdoors" are usually experienced as two distinct environments. By minimizing the walls between these two, we can enhance the potential for learning and develop positive attitudes about the natural world.

Some ways to minimize walls is to take advantage of windows and the natural light they provide. Whenever possible, keep blinds and curtains open, and as weather permits, keep the windows open, as well. Use only transparent displays on windows, and avoid placing objects on windowsills that block the light. Room dividers, book shelves, and other types of furniture or furnishings should be placed strategically so as to avoid blocking light from the windows or views of the outdoors.

Minimizing walls should not be limited to physical walls. Emotional and psychological walls separating us from nature should be minimized, as well. This means addressing such barriers as fear, unfamiliarity, and feelings of disgust. It means thinking of nature not as something "out there" and separate from us, but as something of which we are a part. As expressed by Gary Snyder, "Nature is not a place to visit, it is home" (quoted by Louv, 2011: 157).

# 4

# The role of the adult

Sensitiveness to life is the highest product of education.

(Liberty Hyde Bailey)

Children have an inborn sense of wonder and a strong desire to explore the world around them, yet they need an interested adult to provide encouragement, support, and guidance to keep their spirit of inquiry alive. This adult may be a parent, a naturalist, a teacher, or other caring person in the child's life.

The role of the adult in fostering creative play is less about teaching and more about sharing. As Rachel Carson (1956: 45) says: "If a child is to keep alive his inborn sense of wonder ... he needs the companionship of at least one adult who can share it, rediscovering with him the joy, excitement and mystery of the world we live in." Young children don't learn by having someone telling them about the world around them. They learn and construct meaning through their own physical and mental activities. Children need adults who will support them in their self-initiated explorations and experiments. Well-intentioned parents and teachers aren't always in tune with this. Their attention may be too narrowly focused on what they perceive as safety, health, and cleanliness issues. They may feel, for example, that children should avoid playing in the sand, digging in the dirt, or rolling down the hill. They may tell children to stay away from a water spigot or pump and expect them to keep their hands and clothes from getting dirty. They may discourage children from picking up leaves, dried grasses, or stones. They may feel that children need to be kept indoors when it's rainy, cold, or hot.

Rachel Carson worked from a different perspective. When her nephew, Roger, was about twenty months old, she wrapped him in a blanket and carried him down to the beach. This was on a stormy autumn night – it was dark, and it was rainy. Big waves were thundering against the rocks. Their response to the wild night and their experience of the vast, roaring ocean was to laugh for pure joy. Carson called this a spine-tingling experience and suggested that too many children are "protected" from ever having such experiences. The result, she suggests, is that children may become bored, caught up in the sterile preoccupation with things that are artificial, and alienated from sources of strength.

Some adults may feel that children are natural explorers and thus don't need the guidance and support of adults to benefit from creative outdoor play. They may even feel that outdoor time is "children's time" and that adults should confine their role to keeping children safe. Studies indicate that while adults may be responsive to and interactive with children in indoor settings, their interactions with children tend to be noticeably different while outdoors. While outdoors, teachers use more negative controls, are more sedentary, and engage in less verbal interaction with children (Bilton 2002). A major purpose of this chapter is to encourage adults to view themselves as facilitators of creative play and learning in natural environments.

There are a variety of ways for adults to foster creative play in natural environments. Perhaps the five most important ways are to:

- provide a rich learning environment;
- provide extended periods of uninterrupted time;
- keep the focus on the child;
- model desired attitudes and behaviors;
- interact with the children in a positive way.

## Rich learning environment

Young children should not be placed in environments that are devoid of beauty, variety, and materials that stimulate curiosity and excite the senses. Children depend on sensory stimulation and opportunities for manipulation to learn and grow. They learn about themselves and the world around them by what they experience – not by what they're told. Fostering creative play thus starts by providing an environment in which creativity is fostered.

The teacher or other adult is the manager of the environment. Effective teachers set up an environment that invites and sustains active investigation. They provide materials that can be used in multiple ways and at different levels of sophistication. Most natural materials and art supplies fit this description. Swing sets and slides do not.

"Let nature be the teacher" is a theme that could serve as an overarching principle for fostering creative play in natural environments. Living things and other natural elements are perhaps the most inviting materials for young children. Natural materials are rich in texture and color; they change over time and excite the senses. Natural materials give children rich opportunities to feel, smell, see, hear, and taste. They also tend to be flexible and easily manipulated. They can be used for building and creating magical places. They can be used in collages, weavings, and other artistic expressions.

In addition to making natural materials available, teachers should be generous in introducing a wide variety of other loose parts, as well. Materials should be provided that encourage dramatic play, construction projects, active exploration, and artistic expression.

## Extended periods of uninterrupted time

To benefit from the many opportunities for creative play provided by natural environments, children need long periods of uninterrupted play – and they need this on a daily basis, if possible. They also need time when they are not hurried or directed in their activities. Carson (1956: 68) encourages adults to "take time to listen and talk about the voices of the earth and what they mean – the majestic voice of thunder, the winds, the sound of surf or flowing streams." It takes unhurried time to hear such things, and children should experience them on a frequent basis.

A poetic and beautifully illustrated children's book, *The Other Way to Listen* (Baylor and Parnall 1978), speaks of the importance of spending time in natural environments. In this story, an old man talks to a child about hearing the hills sing, the rocks murmur, and wildflower seeds burst open as they begin to grow underground. The child wants to hear these things, too, so she asks the old man to teach her. His response indicates that nature is the teacher and that it takes a lot of practice and that "you can't be in a hurry." He tells her that most people never hear those things at all because "they just don't take the time you need for something that important." While written as a children's story, *The Other Way to Listen* has important messages for adults, as well, including messages about allowing children extended periods of time in natural environments.

Research on factors influencing positive attitudes towards the environment strongly supports the need for frequent positive experiences in the out-of-doors during childhood. This research focused on "significant life experiences" that influenced individuals to choose professions related to environmental conservation. The top two factors identified are (1) frequent positive experiences in natural environments during childhood; and (2) an adult who modeled interest in and respect for the natural world (Chawla and Hart 1995, Tanner 1980).

Children's lives today tend to be highly programmed and hurried. The environments in which they live and spend their time are becoming more and more homogenized and institutionalized (Crain 2003, Curtis and Carter 2003, Louv 2006). What is missing in the lives of many young children is time to be playful, creative, and thoughtful. Natural environments offer rich opportunities for play, creativity, and reflection. Children should be given the time to benefit from these rich opportunities. Providing this time – and guarding it from intrusions – should be viewed as one of the primary responsibilities of teachers and parents.

## A serene mind

According to Henry David Thoreau, "You cannot perceive beauty, but with a serene mind." To help children appreciate the beauty and wonder of nature, it would be well for adults to model and encourage a "serene mind" while immersed in nature. The best way to do this is to display serenity in what you do and say. At times, you can also invite children to join you in just sitting quietly as you watch the wind blow through the leaves or listen to the birds in the nearby bushes.

You can also foster a serene mind by calling attention to the spiritual or intrinsic aspects of nature, including its aesthetic and interdependent qualities. You might say something like "Just looking at these flowers makes me feel happy" or "Let's sit under the tree for a while. It's such a peaceful place."

## Focus on the child

Most adults are well aware that they need to watch young children closely during outdoor play. Their focus, however, is often limited to safety issues. Without minimizing the importance of safety, close observation should include other essential concerns as well: "What have the children discovered? How are they using materials? How are they interacting with each other? Does one play episode lead to another?" etc.

Close observations of children should also include attention to their interests and fears. Once these areas are identified, it's important for adults to respond appropriately. Identifying children's interests, for example, should be followed up with related comments, materials, and activities. If children show an interest in falling leaves, it would be appropriate to provide rakes, drawing paper and crayons, and books about trees. One teacher – noting children's fascination with raking leaves into "great big piles" – asked them, "How high do you think you can make this pile?" One child suggested "as high as a mountain" – and the challenge was on. The children enthusiastically filled buckets with leaves and emptied them on top of a growing mound of leaves. They started estimating how high or tall the pile might get – as tall as the teacher? As high as the roof overhang? As tall as a tree? They kept pouring buckets of leaves onto the pile. Once they could no longer reach the top of the pile, they asked the teacher to do the pouring.

After the pile got too high for the teacher to reach, one child asked for a ladder. A short ladder was brought onto the scene, and the pouring continued. After that was no longer high enough to reach the top of the pile, the children and teacher sat on the ground and did some "brainstorming" on how they might get more leaves to the top. One inventive child suggested they needed "some kind of a machine" that would take the bucket to the top. The conversation moved on to what this machine might look like. The teacher then challenged the children to draw pictures of the kind of machine that might work. She gave each of them a clipboard, paper, and a pencil, and the children went to work. Their drawings demonstrated a great deal of creative thought and problem-solving ability.

The next day, the teacher provided some simple books on different kinds of machines – especially pulleys and other kinds of "lifters" (moving belts, etc.). This led to more drawings of machines and discussions about how to lift things up. The curriculum in this case emerged from the children's interests. Activities and materials weren't determined by the teacher in advance. Even though the teacher wanted to introduce some fall-related themes, she waited to see what would emerge through the children's interests. This is an example of recognizing that the "curriculum is what happens" when the focus is on the children. It also exemplifies how the curriculum can be child-originated and teacher-framed.

Focusing on the child also means recognizing and respecting children's fears. Some children are afraid of insects, worms, and bugs. They may also be afraid of getting wet or dirty – or being in the dark or hearing thunder. Such fears should not be brushed aside. Some adults seem to think that they can remove a child's fear by simply telling them that there's nothing to be afraid of. This approach doesn't work. Just as young children don't learn about gravity by explaining it to them, so they don't learn to overcome unfounded fears by arguing against the fear. They might be calmed and reassured by the presence and words of a caring adult, but they need another step to overcome their fears. What's often needed is familiarity with that of which they're afraid. Such familiarity, however, should not be forced upon a child.

Jolene, an office manager, recently shared her story about a teacher she had when she was seven years old who inappropriately tried to help her overcome her fear of snakes. A garter snake in a glass cage was a part of the classroom's science center. Children took turns feeding the snake and cleaning its water dish. Jolene never wanted to do this. In fact, she wasn't willing to even stand close to the glass cage. One day, after trying to convince Jolene that she shouldn't be afraid of the snake, the teacher took the snake out of the cage and told Jolene to pet it. Jolene refused. The teacher's response was to drape the snake over Jolene's arm and then tell her: "See, the snake didn't hurt you." No, the snake didn't hurt her, but the experience was traumatic. Jolene's fear of snakes – all kinds of snakes – is with her today. Her immediate reaction when seeing a snake is to flee. Obviously, the teacher's well-intentioned approach to dealing with a child's fear was ineffective. This approach also reflected a lack of sensitivity to and respect for a young child.

A naturalist working with a group of five-year-olds demonstrated a much more positive approach to dealing with children's fears or potential fears. Steve wanted to ignite children's interest in the natural world. When visiting the classroom, he brought a variety of natural materials (pebbles, seeds, dried grasses, flower petals, twigs, etc.). He also brought a live toad. After spending some time with the children and allowing them to manipulate the natural materials, he told them that he had a small animal in the box. He showed the children the holes in the lid to allow air for breathing. He described the toad to the children – four legs, two eyes, soft skin, etc. He showed a picture of the toad and talked about where the toad lived and what it liked to eat. He then asked the children if it would be OK to remove the lid so that they could see the toad. He told them that he would not let the toad out of the box.

After all the children nodded, Steve removed the lid and invited those who wanted to come close and get a better look at the toad. He asked them to talk about what they saw. One child said he could see the toad breathing; another talked about the spots on the toad's skin. Someone noted the "bended legs" and something that "looked like toenails" on the toad. Steve asked the children if it would be OK if he held the toad in his hands so that all the children could get a better view of it. Again, he assured the children that he would keep the toad in his hands. The children gave their consent and, while Steve held the toad, he shared some more information about it – how it hatched from an egg and what kind of food it liked. He then asked the children if they would like to see the toad eat. He said he would have to put the toad down on a dish as he got the food ready. The children gave their permission and Steve fed the toad. He finally asked if anyone wanted to feel the toad's skin. Several children were ready. After they touched the toad and described what it felt like, all the children wanted to touch the toad.

In addition to identifying and responding to children's interests and fears, teachers should also pay close attention to their discoveries and experiences. As children share

**Box 4.1** Open-ended questions
Open-ended questions invite a variety of answers. They can be answered appropriately in multiple ways. They encourage children to think versus just recall.

Examples:
- What would happen if you pour water over the sand?
- Why do you think the leaves are curling?
- Where could we find more seeds?
- What would it feel like to ride on the duck's back?
- How could you make that wall stand up?

what they discover and/or experience, their understanding of what it means deepens. This is especially true if the teacher shows a sincere interest and encourages the children to think about the whys, hows, and what ifs. Open-ended questions represent one of the best ways to do this. An open-ended question allows for many different answers – there's not just a "right" or "wrong" answer. Open-ended questions help children problem-solve and think creatively. They also foster close observation, further conversation, and inquiry. See Box 4.1 for examples of open-ended questions.

Teachers can also respond to children's interests and inquiries by providing related props. Following is an example of how this worked with one group of children. Several children were "camping" in the play yard. A tent had been set up the day before, equipped with some cooking utensils, a knapsack, and binoculars. One child suggested building a fire to cook dinner. The children gathered kindling – dried grasses and sticks. They put some water in a pot and began looking for "vegetables" to make some soup. They found grass, leaves, flower petals, and seeds. They had a plastic knife and decided to cut some of the larger leaves. Andre picked some dandelions and added them to the water. "Hey, my hands are yellow," he said with surprise. The other children looked at their hands and began examining the plant materials more closely.

Maria noticed some green coloring on the board where they had been doing their cutting. "I think you have to cut the grass to get the color out," she said. The focus of the children's activity now turned to "getting the color out."

The teacher had been closely observing the children. She got more plastic knives and some sheets of white paper. She placed these on a nearby table and asked, "Would you like to work over here? You might have more room." Without saying anything more, she placed a red leaf on a sheet of white paper and began to cut the leaf. A red line showed up on the paper. The children began looking for plant materials of different colors. They placed what they found on the white paper and started cutting. They seemed pleased with the results and started planning "designs" versus random marks. As they worked, they noticed the color "comes out" of some materials but not others.

"I bet it just works on soft things – not hard things, like stones," suggested Tina.

"Well, you can't cut a stone, so you can't tell," offered Roger.

"If you had a really strong knife, you could cut a stone – or if you hit it really hard, maybe you could break it," added Andre.

The teacher, who had been listening and watching, posed a question: "Do you have to cut something to get the color out? I didn't see Andre cut the dandelion."

"He was holding the dandelion," said Tina, "but he didn't cut it. What did you do, Andre?"

"I just picked it and put it in the water," answered Andre.

"Did the water get yellow?" asked Maria.

She went over to the pot to look. The water was not yellow.

"So what do you think made the color come out on Andre's hand?" the teacher asked.

"Maybe he squeezed it," suggested Roger. "Did you, Andre?"

"When I picked it, maybe I did," answered Andre.

The children started looking for dandelions. There were just a few in the yard. The children gathered these and brought them over to the table. Some of the children had yellow on their hands, but some didn't. Conversation continued about what made the yellow come out. Roger rubbed his dandelion on a piece of white paper and got a streak of yellow. "I squished it out!" he said.

Other children began squishing dandelions on paper. Tina tried squishing a blade of grass. She got a green smudge on her paper and was delighted. The children began trying different materials. Andre picked up a small stone. "I can't squish it," he said, "but I can rub it." A faint gray-brown line appeared. Everyone seemed pleased.

In this example, the teacher never took the activity away from the children nor did she restructure it to fit preplanned objectives. She had arranged the environment for a "camping" activity. The fact that it led to something else was just fine. She offered encouragement and support, but allowed the children to conduct their own activity. In the process, they constructed their own knowledge and understanding, as well. Both teacher-to-child and child-to-child interactions helped maintain children's focus and led to further investigations and discoveries.

## Attitudes, dispositions, and behaviors

Children learn more from what we do than what we say. Children watch us for information about what is valued, sacred, and important in life. The attitudes, dispositions, and values that children see reflected in the lives of their parents and teachers tend to be the attitudes and values they'll carry with them throughout life. If we want children to be sensitive to and interested in the world of nature, then that's the way we'll have to be. The adult's own sense of wonder – more than his or her scientific knowledge – is what will ignite and sustain a child's love of nature. Rachel Carson (1956: 45), a scientist herself, believes "that for the child, and for the parent [or teacher] seeking to guide him, it is not half so important to know as to feel."

Carson (1956: 52) encourages adults to explore nature with children as partners in exploration and as friends on an expedition of exciting discovery. It's "largely a matter of becoming receptive to what lies all around you," she says. We need to learn again to use our eyes, ears, nostrils, and fingertips to open up "the disused channels of sensory impression."

Adults also need to model caring and respect for the natural environment. Talking to children about taking care of the Earth is far less effective than demonstrating simple ways of expressing care. Care and respect can be modeled through the gentle handling of plants and animals in the classroom and outdoors, establishing and maintaining outdoor habitats for wildlife, attending to the responsible disposal of trash, and recycling or reusing as many materials as possible.

## Positive interactions

Teachers sometimes feel that once an ample supply of materials is available and organized, their job in supporting creative play is finished. They view children as competent, naturally curious, and eager to learn, and thus mistakenly feel that children can be left on their own. While their view of children is generally correct, teachers need to realize that young children's skills in exploring, experimenting, and collaborating are not refined. Children need support and lots of practice to further develop their skills in all the developmental domains. Without sufficient adult support, the creative play of many young children will be of short duration and cursory in nature.

Generally, children left alone to play do not develop imaginatively. Their play behavior becomes repetitive and fails to progress in complexity and creativity (Bilton 2002). Left alone, children may also engage in play that reinforces stereotypical ideas and behaviors (e.g. only males can be firefighters, only females can feed the baby, etc.). Teachers shouldn't hesitate to participate in play to challenge prejudice as it arises – unless another child does this. Research indicates that stereotypical play is reduced when adults get involved in children's play (Bilton 2002).

Adults provide support for creative play by showing interest and interacting with the children to the extent necessary to keep them actively involved for a period of time. While respecting the fact that the play belongs to the children, adults can extend and enrich the play experience by being physically close, asking related open-ended questions, making positive comments, adding appropriate props, and sometimes entering into a supportive role during dramatic play.

Adults need to take care, however, to carefully assess children's intent before becoming actively involved in the children's project. It's good to ask about a project or pretend event before offering suggestions or providing information. What a child is trying to do may be quite different from what an adult assumes to be the focus of the activity. For example, an adult may make a comment about the "garden" a child is cultivating. The child's intent, however, may be more along the lines of planting grass for their horse to eat. "You've been working really hard over here. Would you like to tell me about your project?" is one way to solicit information about the child's intent.

Adults can also provide opportunities for children to share their ideas and projects with others. Such opportunities often challenge children to think more deeply about what they're doing and may lead to a productive exchange of ideas among the children.

At times, children may get frustrated and angry if their projects aren't working as they envisioned. They will then need adult support to help them define and solve the problem. The definition of the problem and ideas on how to solve it should come from the children – not offered by the adult. "You seem to be having trouble. Can you tell me what's going on?" is one way to get the conversation – and the problem-solving – started. In group play, children may have trouble finding a meaningful role for everyone. Here, adults can help by asking questions or making suggestions (e.g. "Do you need someone to order a pizza?" or "Maybe Sonia could hold the bucket while you pour the sand.").

In interacting with children during creative play activities, teachers should keep in mind the principle of "least intrusive involvement" (Kostelnik *et al.* 2007). This principle is based on the idea of providing only the level of support actually needed to extend children's engagement in an activity. Active onlooking is the least intrusive level and physical intervention the most.

Basing adult intervention on the principle of "least intrusive involvement" is generally the most effective way to support creative play and active problem-solving on the part of the children. Adults must, therefore, determine the level of support needed by an individual child or group of children. Younger children and children with disabilities will often require more intrusive interventions than children with more developed play skills. Reticent children may also require a higher level of support and over a longer period of time (Bilton 2002). Teachers need to be especially attentive and responsive to the social and emotional needs of children to determine the level of support that is needed.

> Sometimes you are needed right in the thick of things to model and coach communication skills, the collaborative process, and problem solving. At other times your involvement might send the wrong message – that you don't value or trust what children are doing.
>
> (Curtis and Carter 2003: 186)

At times, children need more direct teaching to develop the technical skills needed to use certain materials effectively (scissors, for example). Keep in mind that showing a child how to use materials appropriately doesn't always impede creativity (Kostelnik *et al.* 2007). On the contrary, lack of skill can impede creativity and be frustrating to the child. Thus, teachers can show children how to use scissors or a hole punch. They can also show children how much glue to use and where to put it. Generally, telling the children what to paint or expecting them to model their projects on the teacher's example are not appropriate.

The adult's role is to prepare the environment and then provide information, ideas, encouragement, and resources on an "as needed" basis. When intervention is necessary, it should be as least intrusive and as short in duration as possible. Teachers should have a clear understanding of why they are joining in the children's play and how they think this will help the children (Bilton 2002).

## What not to do

Some adults may feel a need to "teach" while they're outdoors with children. They may conduct teacher-led activities and provide labels and explanations in their attempts to describe the world of nature. This approach isn't developmentally appropriate for young children and works against creativity, curiosity, and appreciation of self and the natural world.

Rachel Carson's approach is a much better match to how young children learn. She says that the sharing of nature with children should be "based on having fun together rather than on teaching" (Carson 1956: 10). Thus, adults should not feel intimidated if they don't know the names of native plants and animals; nor should they try to conduct frequent teacher-directed lessons while outdoors with young children.

Adults should also avoid teaching young children "to save the Earth." It's tempting because of the damage humans have done to the Earth. We want the next generation to be better stewards of the environment. So we wonder whether we should tell young children that the future of the planet is in jeopardy and that they must somehow fix it. While most early childhood educators would say, "Of course not," such attempts are not uncommon. Consider the following nursery rhyme adapted from "Humpty Dumpty":

> All the people sat on the wall. All the people had a great fall. All the pollution and all the trash made the whole Earth crash.

This is just one example of what a teacher wrote who felt she was doing the right thing – she wanted to teach the children to "save the Earth." While we want children to be interested in the natural world and to understand simple ways in which they can contribute to keeping the Earth clean and healthy, we should avoid working from a fear approach. Nor do we want to place a heavy and unfair burden on young children.

Placing the burden of the world's ecological problems on young children leads to "ecophobia" – a fear of environmental tragedies (Sobel 2004a). The result is an alienation from nature instead of a positive connection with it. One of the goals of creative play in natural environments is to instill a sense of appreciation for the natural world. Instilling fear is counterproductive to achieving this goal.

Ecophobia creates havoc with both the natural environment and the spirit and soul of humankind. Physical manifestations of ecophobia include strip mines, deforestation, polluted lakes and streams, and toxic air. Psychological and spiritual results of ecophobia include anxiety, depression, and a shrinking range of experiences and joys in daily life.

Ecophobia can develop through inappropriate environmental education initiatives. Early childhood environmental education that emphasizes the loss of species, polluted air and water, and other environmental disasters are not in the best interests of the child – nor are they effective in fostering a love and respect for the natural world. Information about environmental tragedies and concerns is developmentally inappropriate with young children and tends to be counterproductive in fostering an environmental ethic.

Sobel (2004a) indicates that when we neglect the developmental aspects of environmental education and introduce environmental tragedies too early, we end up alienating children from nature. In fostering an environmental ethic, it's wise to keep Rachel Carson's (1956: 45) words in mind:

> The years of early childhood are the time to prepare the soil ... It is more important to pave the way for the child to want to know than to put him on a diet of facts he is not ready to assimilate.

# 5

# Holistic child development

Environments for young children should be designed with the healthy development of the whole child in mind. This requires attention to each of the developmental domains as well as to the child's emerging curiosity, imagination, and sense of wonder. For fostering the development of the whole child, there's probably nothing more effective than playing and learning in natural environments.

## Domain-related skills

The developmental domains of childhood include adaptive, aesthetic, cognitive, social, emotional, and physical. Creative play in natural environments promotes development in each of these areas.

## Adaptive skills

Adaptive skills have to do with how well a child can adapt to and function independently in his or her environment. Natural outdoor settings offer variety, challenges, and innumerable sources of motivation. Such settings provide the child with opportunities for applying skills learned in a more structured setting to one that is more unstructured. Indoors, children may practice placing blocks on a shelf with the expectation of some order and within a specified "clean up time." Outdoors, children may form a circle of stones around a flower bed. In each case (i.e. with the blocks and with the stones), the children are picking up objects and arranging them in an orderly way. Indoors, the task is predetermined – the blocks are to be returned to the shelf after play time. "There's a place for everything; and everything goes in its place" is a fairly typical understanding in classroom settings. Outdoors, however, the rules are often more relaxed. Loose parts are meant to be manipulated and moved about. They can be used for a variety of purposes and left in different places. The stones that outline the flower bed one day may be the "load" in a bucket or wagon the next day. Natural loose parts (stones, seeds, leaves, etc.) don't have to be "put away" at the end of a play period. Yet, the adaptive skill of picking up objects and placing them in an orderly way is still practiced.

Children are usually more motivated to practice adaptive skills outdoors than indoors. The unstructured aspect of a natural environment serves as one source of motivation. The "fun factor" is certainly another source.

"Asking for help" is another adaptive skill that young children need to develop. Situations outdoors that may motivate young children to ask for help could include the need for assistance in climbing a tree, maintaining balance while walking through a snow drift, and attaching a hose to a water spigot.

## Aesthetic development

Aesthetics can be defined as sensitivity to beauty in nature and art. Such sensitivity is fostered not by talking about beauty but by experiencing it in a variety of forms – brilliantly colored leaves on a maple tree, the scent of earth after a rain, the singing of birds, and the softness of a kitten's fur. The natural world – with its incredibly rich sources of sensory stimulation – provides innumerable opportunities to experience beauty. It's thus easy to see how nature can serve as an ideal resource for the aesthetic development of young children.

An early snowfall in winter may provide a child with his or her first remembered experience of snow. Seeing a rainbow in the sky may be something a three-year-old has never experienced before, and watching a butterfly move from flower to flower may provide a visual feast the child has not yet come to take for granted.

Adults can support children's aesthetic development by commenting on various aspects of the natural environment. They might make such comments as, "There are so many colors in the sky today" and "I like the feel of these leaves; they're so leathery." Such comments encourage children to look at the world around them more closely and to be aware of its aesthetic qualities. Adults can also encourage children to visually represent what they observe and experience in the natural world through such creative expressions as drawing, painting, and dancing. Representations have a beauty of their own and help children appreciate the aesthetic qualities of the subject, process, and product of artistic expression.

## Cognitive development

The natural world also offers many opportunities for cognitive development. Manipulating natural materials helps children learn about the physical characteristics of the world around them. They learn – through experience – the difference between the hardness of a rock and the softness of grass. They learn about the properties of water in its different forms (liquid, ice, and vapor) and the sturdiness of a tree when compared with the fragility of a spider's web. Through experimentation, they discover that some things float and others sink, that birds like some seeds more than others, and that a bucket of sand is heavier than a bucket of leaves.

Young children also develop cognitively by using all their senses – in fact, "the more experiences children have with their senses, the more knowledge they gain" (Theemes 1999: 19). Fortunately, natural outdoor environments provide many opportunities for children to experience all the senses: visual, kinesthetic, tactile, auditory, smell, and taste. The following examples provide just a small sampling of how the natural world stimulates the senses.

- Visual stimulation comes from interesting shapes, colors, and forms found so readily in such natural materials as plants, soil, water, and sand.
- The kinesthetic sense influences children's spatial awareness and helps them understand the relationship of their physical self to the environment. This sense also influences children's eye–hand and eye–foot coordination and plays a role in developing a sense of balance and coordination. Trees, logs, rocks, small nooks, different ground elevations, bridges, bushes, benches, steps, and trails invite children to develop their kinesthetic sense through such activities as climbing, rolling, jumping, crawling, and bending.
- The tactile sense has to do with touch and involves the entire surface of the body. The outdoor setting stimulates the tactile sense in a wide variety of ways – temperatures vary from hot to cold, wind moves air across a child's skin, the textures of plant materials vary from soft to hard and smooth to rough, soil can be moist or dry, hard or soft, etc. Encouraging children to dig in the dirt, play with sand, experiment with water, collect natural materials, and spend time outdoors in a variety of weather conditions will stimulate their tactile sense and develop new understandings about the natural world.
- Children's auditory sense is stimulated as they listen to different sounds. Natural environments provide a wide variety of sounds that children may not be exposed to while indoors – birds chirping, water dripping, leaves rustling, branches rubbing against other, etc. While outdoors, children should be encouraged to focus on and identify the different sounds around them. Children can also make simple musical instruments with natural materials. This will offer additional auditory stimulation and help children tune in to their auditory sense. Wind chimes might be added, as well.
- Children's sense of smell can be stimulated in a variety of ways during outdoor play. Plants with interesting scents should be close to where children play. Such plants can include flowers, herbs, and fruit trees. Children can also explore different scents by rubbing or crushing leaves and grasses.
- The sense of taste should also be stimulated through outdoor play but under the careful supervision of an adult. Young children will have a tendency to taste plant parts and maybe even mud. The first line of defense in keeping children safe from ingesting materials that may be harmful to them is making sure there are no toxins washing into the children's play area and that none of the plants are poisonous. Children should also be instructed not to taste anything without first asking an adult. Adults can stimulate the sense of taste in the outdoor environment by providing healthy snacks and an inviting gathering place outdoors to enjoy the snacks. Children can be involved in the preparation of such snacks (e.g. making sandwiches, cleaning fruit, etc.). Involving children in

the cultivation and harvesting of a small vegetable garden is another excellent way of stimulating the sense of taste. Gardening with children has many other benefits, as well, including helping children learn about healthy foods and where such foods come from. Gardening can also promote children's self-esteem and sense of competence.

## Social development

Establishing and enjoying relationships with others is the overall goal of social skill development. To reach this goal, children must learn to communicate effectively, regulate their behaviors within the norms of societal expectations, and discover their place in a variety of group settings. Social competence is manifested in the way "children perceive, interpret, and respond to the variety of social situations they encounter. ... A high level of social competence in our society means that a person exhibits responsible, independent, friendly, cooperative, purposeful, and self-controlled behavior" (Kostelnik *et al.* 2007: 351).

Creative play in natural environments offers rich opportunities for social skill development. In using natural materials, children have many opportunities to share their discoveries, to negotiate and problem-solve with others, and to make and enjoy playing with friends. They also have the opportunity to practice pro-social behaviors such as helping and cooperating. As they interact with others, children learn effective communication skills, as well.

Communication skills – so essential to social development – aren't developed in a vacuum. Communication occurs only in relationships and requires the giving and receiving of a message. "Communication needs to be two-way. Teachers need to communicate 'with' children not 'to' children" (Basile and White 2000: 58). The outdoor environment is the ideal place to engage in dialogue with children, as there are so many interesting and ever-changing topics for discussion.

Motivation is the thrust behind attempts to communicate. Young children learning language need something worth communicating about – they need a message they consider important enough for the thought and energy it takes to share it with others. The natural world offers innumerable possibilities for stimulating children's interest in sharing their experiences and discoveries with others.

It's interesting that the first word Helen Keller understood in her process of learning to communicate was "water." Helen was deaf and blind. Her teacher, Ann Sullivan, had been trying without much success to teach Helen to communicate by spelling out words in her hand. Helen did not fully understand the meaning of words. All this changed, however, when Ann led Helen to a water pump as someone was drawing water. Ann placed one of Helen's hands under the spout while she spelled the word "water" in her other hand. Helen later recounted the incident:

As the cool stream gushed over one hand she [Ann] spelled into the other the word water, first slowly, then rapidly. I stood still, my whole attention fixed upon the motions of her fingers. Suddenly I felt a misty consciousness ... and somehow the mystery of language was revealed to me.

(Royal National Institute of the Blind, n.d.)

Within the next few hours, Helen learned the spelling of thirty new words and fully understood what they meant.

Perhaps it was the rich sensory experience of water gushing over her hand that helped Helen make the connection between the word as it was spelled in her hand and the water itself. It's not hard to think of water gushing over her hand as far more stimulating than feeling a spoon or brush placed in her hand.

Water, like so many other natural elements and materials, is sensory and provides a variety of sensory experiences. We see that children are drawn to water – they're fascinated by its "wetness," its force, the different forms it can take, its way of "carrying things" and "holding things up," and the way it seeps through dirt, sand, and cloth. Other natural materials, too, tend to be multidimensional and can be experienced in a variety of ways. Such things as twigs, shells, stones, leaves, and other natural materials make excellent language-development props as children are motivated to communicate ideas and experiences that stimulate their senses and excite their imagination.

## Emotional development

Attending to the emotional development of children is a critical, but subtle, aspect of teaching. Part of the challenge relates to the fact that the emotional development of children is predominantly an internal process. This makes it difficult to track (Theemes 1999). While external events and experiences influence our emotions, internal states play a role, as well. Emotions – while experienced as both positive (e.g. joy, excitement, love) and negative (e.g. anger, jealousy, sadness) – shouldn't be viewed as good or bad. It's the expression of the emotions that can be evaluated in relation to what is appropriate and healthy or inappropriate and unhealthy.

Children's emotions should never be dismissed or denied. Their joy, excitement, fear, anger, etc. should be acknowledged. What children need in the process of developing emotional competence is help in understanding their emotions and guidance on how to express such emotions in socially appropriate and personally healthy ways.

While socio-emotional development was at one time viewed as a single developmental domain, emotional competence is now being recognized as an area of development that is separate from (yet related to) social competence (Garner and Estep 2001). Emotional competence, as an area of child development, has long been underrated, but this is changing (Denham 2001). New understandings about the impact of emotional competence to other areas of development indicate that "when developmental milestones of emotional competence are not negotiated successfully, children are at risk, both at the time and later in life" (Denham 2001: 5). Areas of concern relating to emotional development include behavioral difficulties, the development of a sense of well-being, and the ability to learn effectively (Denham 2001, Roffey and O'Reirdan 2001).

Emotionally competent children know how to vary their behavior to correspond with the thoughts, feelings, and situations of those around them. They are also less likely to be involved in angry disputes with peers and more likely to use constructive strategies in response to potentially conflicting situations. They are also more likely to be popular with their peers than children who are not emotionally competent.

The lack of emotional competence tends to promote "spiralling difficulties" in children's ability to interact and form healthy relationships with others (Denham 2001).

Children's emotional competence and their ability to learn and be successful in a classroom setting are also related. Research studies have shown that deficiencies in emotional competence include not only disruptive behaviors but also poor school performance (Roffey and O'Reirdan 2001, Shields *et al.* 2001). Children who are unable to monitor and modulate their emotional arousal usually find it very difficult (or impossible) to maintain an optimal level of engagement within the school context (Shields *et al.* 2001). They tend to have trouble regulating their own behavior, adjusting to classroom structure, complying with rules and limits, and negotiating cooperative relationships with their peers.

Garner and Estep's work (2001), on the other hand, indicates that children who are knowledgeable about emotions and able to control the expression of emotions in the classroom are more likely to perform better on cognitive tasks than other children. Other research studies found that preschoolers' emotional regulation at the start of the school year was associated with higher achievement at the end of the year, whereas early emotional liability predicted poorer outcomes (Shields *et al.* 2001).

To appropriately guide young children in the development of emotional competence, teachers need to be aware of related expectations at different stages of development. A list of skills and abilities that can be expected of most five-year-old children who are developing emotionally at an optimum rate may be helpful. Some of these skills and abilities are presented in Box 5.1.

As in other areas of development, efforts to foster emotional competence should focus on building strengths versus fixing deficiencies. As Denham (2001: 5) states:

**Box 5.1**  Indicators of emotional competence in five-year-old children

- being enthusiastic and motivated to learn;
- experiencing a wide range of feelings (but not necessarily able to identify them clearly);
- being aware of feelings and able to relate these to wants;
- uses a range of varied, complex, and flexible ways of expressing emotions;
- uses language for emotional control and expression;
- has increasing emotional control (but not able to hide feelings completely);
- uses play to work out emotional issues;
- demonstrates a growing sensitivity to the feelings of others;
- cares about pets and younger children;
- comforts distressed peers;
- identifies what is right and wrong in relation to family and cultural values;
- tests behavioral boundaries from time to time.

These indicators are based on the work of Roffey and O'Reirdan (2001). Indicators for additional ages can be accessed online at http://www.pbs.org/wholechild/abc/social.html

"We owe our children more than a mere lack of disorder, more than averting tragedy. We need to study not just weakness, but also strength, not just fixing what is broken, but nurturing what is best within our children." Teachers and other adults can play a key role in fostering children's emotional competence. They can do this by coaching children in such areas as (1) recognizing different emotions and their manifestations; (2) coping with frustration; (3) understanding different situations; and (4) viewing situations from someone else's perspective (Shields *et al.* 2001). While "coaching interventions" (which tend to be somewhat didactic) have proven effective, studies examining teachers' naturally occurring influences indicate that preschoolers' secure emotional attachments to their teachers also impact children's display of emotions in school. Young children who develop secure attachments to their teachers are less likely to engage in unregulated anger and behavior problems. They are also more likely to exhibit positive emotions in the school setting (Shields *et al.* 2001). A warm, close relationship between child and teacher, then, can positively influence young children's emerging emotional competence.

There are many naturally occurring opportunities for children to learn how to deal with the frustration of mastering a new academic skill, negotiating the complex behaviors involved in sharing and cooperating, and managing angry feelings when limits are placed on their behaviors. While teachers should certainly capitalize on these naturally occurring situations, they should also seriously consider the importance of establishing strong relationships with young children as a vehicle for fostering emotional competence.

Research and theory – especially in the area of ecopsychology – indicate that positive experiences with the natural environment are also important to emotional development (Louv 2006). In addition to having an innate affinity with the natural world, humans also have an emotional and psychological need to care for things outside themselves. This need can be met – and human life enriched – by caring for the world of nature.

Attachment to nature should not be viewed as a luxury – it's a "key to health and well-being throughout childhood" (Bohling-Phillippi 2006: 51). The emotional benefits of interacting with nature include reduced stress, healthy sense of well-being, and increased attention span (Bohling-Phillippi 2006, Louv 2006).

Nurturing activities, such as caring for flowers, trees, worms, or classroom pets, can also help children who are angry or hurting. Focusing negative energy on positive activities helps to restore the human spirit. For young children, caring for some other living thing can help them develop a sense of themselves as nurturers (Bohling-Phillippi 2006).

Creative play in natural environments should always be guided by a sense of respect for living things and a genuine concern for nature. Concern for wild creatures and their habitats tends to promote greater fulfillment in one's individual life and possibly a sense of caring for other people. Positive experiences in natural environments also tend to foster a healthy self-concept, an internal locus of control, improved personal and social adjustment, and an enhanced perception of self (Elliot 2008).

Without frequent positive experiences in natural environments, children tend to manifest some unhealthy emotional/psychological states, such as depression and anxiety. Richard Louv (2006), in *The Last Child in the Woods*, refers to this condition as "nature–deficit disorder" and suggests it includes a narrowing of the senses – physiologically and psychologically – and reduces the richness of the human experience. Louv also suggests that the dramatic increase in attention deficit diagnoses may be related to the rapid pace of our electronic culture. For emotional and psychological wellness, children need to be in frequent contact with the slower rhythms of the natural world.

The joy of teaching and learning is often experienced more in the context of emotional connections than through intellectual pursuits. Teaching – when it focuses on the holistic development of children – is a sacred activity. "It's also an exquisitely human activity" (Wilson 2003a: 27). Holistic teaching in natural settings should include time for reflection, discussion, and honest expression. This approach promotes deep connections between teacher and children, and between children and the natural world. These connections, in turn, both reflect and foster healthy emotional development.

## Physical development

Most outdoor playspaces invite a wide variety of physical activities and promote the development of large motor skills. Such skills include (1) locomotor skills (walking, running, leaping, hopping, skipping, rolling, etc.); (2) manipulative skills (throwing, bouncing, catching, kicking, etc.); and (3) nonlocomotor skills (bending, lifting, swaying, turning, swinging, etc.) (Kostelnik *et al.* 2007). No other environment – except perhaps a well-equipped gym – offers such a variety of opportunities for physical development.

As children engage in physical activities, they're developing not only large motor skills, but also other related skills, as well, such as spatial awareness, sense of balance, and perceptual–motor skills. They're also developing a sense of self-efficacy. Self-efficacy refers to one's judgment of what he or she can do with the skills possessed. Self-efficacy can be observed as children make choices about how high to climb or how long to try specific tasks (e.g. riding a tricycle). A child with high self-efficacy may climb to the highest platform on a play structure and slide down the longest pole. He or she may also make repeated attempts to hit or catch a ball. Children with low self-efficacy doubt their abilities and may not try new skills or quit trying easily.

A strong sense of self-efficacy is something that adults should encourage in young children. This doesn't mean forcing children into activities that frighten them or that they're not ready for. Children should be given the freedom to explore, observe, and imitate. They should also be given the gift of time – to determine on their own when they're ready for a bigger challenge. Adults should neither rush the process nor hold the children back. Children have an urge for independence and achievement. This urge can be highly motivating, and children are inclined to challenge themselves. Yet, they will usually go only as far as they feel safe.

"Movement is about self-discovery" (Bilton 2002: 115). As children move their bodies, they find out what they can do – what physical skills they've developed and different ways in which they can use these skills. This discovery increases their self-respect and self-worth. "They will then go on to try new and challenging movements and so the cycle of confidence moves upwards" (Bilton 2002: 115).

**Photograph 5.1**   Adventurous nature play

Children's sense of self-efficacy can be damaged by being overly cautious. Of course, it's important that playspaces are reasonably safe for the ages of the children using them and that adults remain nearby and attentive while children try their skills. One role of the adult is to make sure that young children are not crowded or pushed by others. A child may know, for example, that they can climb safely to the top of a jungle gym by holding tight to the structure. If pushed by another child, however, they may lose their grip and balance. Such accidents not only put children at risk of injury but can also negatively affect their sense of confidence and self-efficacy, as well.

Outdoor environments play an important role in fostering good health and physical fitness. Exercise – which is an almost constant part of outdoor play for many children – increases deep breathing and oxygen intake. Exercise also aids the functioning of all the body's inner systems (respiratory, circulatory, digestive, and eliminative) and can prevent obesity.

While the need for physical fitness may become evident as children grow older, its importance at the early childhood level should not be minimized. "Young children who are fit continue to maintain their fitness in adolescence" (Kostelnik *et al.* 2007: 331). It's important for young children to enjoy physical activity and see it as an ordinary and ongoing part of their lives.

One way to support health and fitness in a natural environment is to encourage such outdoor sports-related activities as running, biking, and playing ball. To make these activities developmentally appropriate and enjoyable for all the children, it's best to keep these activities and games non-competitive. Remember that children will have many opportunities to play competitively as they get older. In group games, children should be encouraged to perform at their best, but not at the expense of someone else. One child or one group of children should not be pitted against another. The focus should be on cooperation rather than competition.

A lifelong interest in fitness can also be encouraged by role playing different types of outdoor recreation activities – camping, hiking, canoeing, etc. Outdoor dramatic play areas might include a tent, canoe, binoculars, walking sticks, etc. Stories about people engaging in such activities might also be shared.

## Wonder, creativity, and imagination

Research indicates that children living close to nature tend to experience it as a source of wonder, joy, and awe. This differs from the way most adults know the world. Children's way of knowing the world is deep and profound; it tends to be more intuitive and in touch with the essence of the natural world. The uniqueness of the childhood experience is manifested, in part, by the child's ability to "experience the natural environment in a deep and direct manner, not as a background for events, but rather, as a factor and stimulator" (Sebba 1991: 395). The unique affinity that children have for the environment usually decreases as the child gets older. This seems to be especially true in Western cultures where there is a tendency to base understandings about the natural world on cognitive representations (i.e. models that we construct) rather than on an ongoing investigation and experience of nature as a complex entity full of mystery and wonder (Carson 1956, Sebba 1991).

It's a mistake to channel children's understandings of the natural world to cognitive representations or theoretical models. This approach leaves children with only limited knowledge about the world. Fuller understandings call for imagination and wonder. This was recognized centuries ago by the philosopher Plato, who indicated that wonder is the source of knowledge. Edith Cobb (1977), in her highly visionary book *The Ecology of Imagination in Childhood*, suggested the same – that it is through wonder that we come to know the world. Wonder, she says, is the wellspring of knowledge; it is also the basis of creativity and imagination.

Adults can support wonder, creativity, and imagination by providing tools for exploration, experimentation, and representation: binoculars, magnifying glasses, clipboards, writing/drawing utensils, collection boxes, display shelves, digging tools, spray bottles, etc. Rather than focusing on "teaching" children about the natural world, adults should focus on developing an awareness and enjoyment of the beauty and wonder of nature.

Wonder, creativity and imagination cannot be taught. They come by way of experience, insight, and personal discovery. Following are some guidelines and suggestions for supporting this process:

- Begin with simple experiences.
- Keep children actively involved.
- Provide pleasant, memorable experiences.
- Emphasize experiencing versus teaching.
- Engage full use of the senses.
- Demonstrate a personal interest in and enjoyment of the natural world.
- Maintain a warm, accepting, and nurturing atmosphere.
- Focus on the beauty and wonder of nature.

# Begin with simple experiences

"Overloading" is a dangerous practice in many fields of endeavor, including education. In helping young children learn about themselves and the world around them, the best place to start is with what is simple and familiar to them. This approach will help children feel comfortable and secure.

Opportunities for young children to interact with the natural world are rapidly decreasing. Many children come to school and other educational settings (e.g. nature centers, etc.) with little or no direct experience with natural environments. They may, thus, have little understanding and unfounded fears about what might happen to them in their encounters with nature. They may fear the darkness of a wooded area. They may think that all bugs and insects bite or sting. In their minds, an earthworm may be a poisonous snake. Such children need gradual, gentle exposure to the world of nature. They need to become familiar with the trees and bushes in the schoolyard before they'll feel comfortable walking in the woods. They'll have to observe and help care for classroom pets before they're asked to accept a caterpillar or ladybug crawling across their hand. They need to know that the natural world is a safe place to be and to play.

Following are some examples of what it means to start with simple activities:

- watching a bean seed or grass seed sprout in a cup before attempting to plant a larger garden;
- playing with snow or leaves in the texture table before making and crawling through tunnels of snow or piles of leaves in the yard;
- watching birds and squirrels from a "window on nature" before suggesting that a pony or calf eats from their hands;
- walking barefoot in the grass or sand before wading in a shallow stream.

# Keep children actively involved

Young children learn most effectively when they are actively engaged, rather than in merely receptive or passive activities. Active engagement should include interactions with adults, materials, and other aspects of their surroundings.

To keep children actively involved, teachers should serve as facilitators, enablers, and consultants (Harlan 1992). As facilitators, teachers create a learning environment that is inviting and responsive. Such an environment may be one in which children are allowed to be messy and get messy. It invites exploration and experimentation, and lets the children know that they are competent.

As enablers, teachers help children become aware of themselves as thinkers and problem-solvers (Harlan 1992). Rather than trying to be the ultimate source of knowledge, teachers view their role as helping children realize that they can discover (or construct) their own knowledge. Enablers share the excitement of discovery with the children and value the process of experimenting and exploring as much as (or more than!) the outcome.

As consultants, teachers observe carefully, listen closely, and answer questions simply (Harlan 1992). The teacher supports rather than directs the child's learning.

It is the child's interest, curiosity, and need to know that set the agenda and drive the activity. While the teacher may introduce the idea of watching a bird gather materials to make a nest, children's unanticipated interest in ants on the sidewalk should be attended to and supported. It is far better to foster a sense of wonder through what the children find of interest than to work from an "instructor's mode" and attempt to teach facts about what the teacher planned in advance.

## Provide pleasant, memorable experiences

Children develop a lifelong interest in learning through experiences that are pleasant and memorable – not through experiences that are forced or dull. They get "hooked on learning" once they discover that they can have a good time through the process. For this reason, the "do not touch" approach to teaching and learning will never work with young children. They want to hold and manipulate. They'll reach out to pick flowers, dig in the dirt, and splash in the water.

Of course, we may not always want the flowers picked or the vegetables harvested before they're ready. Instead of just saying "no," we should find other interesting ways for the children to be actively engaged. We might provide a spray bottle with water to give the plants a drink. We might suggest using a hand lens to examine the leaves more closely or a camera (pretend or real) to take a picture of a flowering plant. The important thing is to keep the activities fun and interesting. Unless children can appreciate (and enjoy) the activities themselves, they will not appreciate the object or idea we're attempting to introduce. Teachers would do well, then, to expend as much thought and energy in considering the "enjoyment factor" of an activity or experience as they do on the "content factor."

## Emphasize experiencing versus teaching

For optimal learning, young children need to be involved in sharing and doing versus listening and watching. They need to explore, experiment, and follow their own curiosity and ideas. The teacher's role is not to give the children information but to provide opportunities for them to experience the richness of the natural environment.

Children are naturally curious. They seek information about their environment and, if encouraged or supported, actively experiment with materials available to them. A wise teacher will encourage children to experiment, explore, and get into things that are safe. Effective teachers also provide a variety of materials and tools.

Wise teachers understand that when children ask "What's that?" they aren't always looking for the name of something. In fact, giving them a name (e.g. "ladybug") may end the conversation and investigation. The effective teacher will realize that providing a simple answer may cut short further observation and thought. A better response would be to pose other questions for the children to consider – questions for which children can seek their own answers. Examples: Is it alive? How does it move? Do you see any eyes, nose, mouth, ears, etc.? What do you think it eats? Such questions help children enter more fully into the experience of being and learning in a natural environment.

# Engage full use of the senses

Children need many and varied opportunities for experiencing the natural world through their senses. "Immersing techniques" are sometimes used to help children become sensorily more in touch with the natural world. Some "immersing techniques" suggested by Van Matre (1990) include:

- Take off some articles of clothing (e.g. shoes and socks) to increase physical contact.
- Crawl or roll on the ground instead of walking.
- Simulate natural processes through bodily movements (e.g. move like the wind, float like a cloud, etc.).
- Temporarily block the sense of sight or sound to heighten the other senses.
- Pet and hug and kiss selected things in nature (e.g. a tree, flower, or stone).

Immersing techniques help children see, hear, touch, taste, and smell the world of nature. Such techniques help tap into a sixth sense, as well. This sixth sense is intuition and is often overlooked as a way of knowing the world. Intuition is the sense that helps a child "feel" the natural world more deeply and personally, and "absorb" its various moods and meanings. Intuition is the direct or immediate perception of truths, facts, concepts, etc. without relying on reasoning. One "truth" often experienced through intuition is a sense of a personal relationship (or friendship) with the natural world. Acknowledging what children discover through intuition is one way to help them feel at home with the world of nature. A child's declaration that the wind kissed their cheek or that the branches of a bush gave them a hug should never be dismissed. Nature has the power to touch us in a variety of ways, and these ways warrant respect.

What children experience and discover through their senses will often be paired with rational thought (Harlan 1992). Children offering their own versions of why certain events occur in the natural world often provide examples of the pairing of intuitive and rational thinking. A child may describe the sudden movement of a breeze through leaves as the tree's way of saying "good-bye." Some teachers may be tempted to use this as a "teachable moment" to provide a lesson on the properties of wind. Wise teachers – in tune with young children and their way of thinking – encourage the child to wave back.

# Demonstrate a personal interest in and enjoyment of the natural world

The teacher's authentic interest and enjoyment are critical to promoting young children's positive engagement with the natural world. It's the teacher's own sense of wonder that will ignite and sustain the young child's interest and involvement with nature. Teachers with a minimum background in science sometimes feel intimidated by the thought of helping children learn about the natural world. These teachers can feel at ease, as there are many ways to foster close observation and hands-on involvement with nature without knowing many of the scientific facts about the way nature works.

Following are just a few suggestions:

- Provide a special place to display natural materials (pine cones, shiny pebbles, seeds, snake skins, etc.).
- Involve children in growing plants from seeds or bulbs.
- Provide books and pictures depicting the beauty, diversity, and wonder of nature.
- Take time to closely examine with the children different types of plants, rocks, trees, insects, etc.
- Invite naturalists to share information about nature.
- Set up and maintain a bird feeder or bird bath.

Young children learn more about attitudes and values from their observations of adults' behaviors than they do from what adults say. If an adult takes the time to watch a butterfly move from flower to flower or a squirrel eat corn from a cob, children's curiosity and respect are likely to be aroused. If, however, the teacher walks right by and never seems to notice the beauty and wonder of nature, the children are likely to dismiss the sounds, sights, and feel of nature as having little importance. It is the teacher's enthusiasm and interest in nature – more than his or her scientific knowledge about the natural world – that will have the greatest impact on arousing children's curiosity and engagement.

Teachers can show enthusiasm and interest in nature by stopping to look, to feel, and to listen. They can kneel on the ground and put their face in the grass to enjoy the scent of a wildflower growing there. They can use a magnifying glass to examine the many colors of a small pebble or the webbing of a leaf. They can pause in what they're doing to watch as a flock of geese makes its way south for the winter.

Once a teacher demonstrates a sense of wonder and interest in nature, these same qualities are likely to be "caught" by children. Much of what we want children to learn or develop through their early childhood years is not so much taught as it is caught. This is especially true when it comes to knowing and appreciating the world of nature. To show respect and appreciation for the natural world, teachers should lead the way in practicing ecologically responsible behaviors, such as:

- actively caring for plants and animals;
- using only as much water and other materials as needed;
- planting flowers, trees, and a variety of native plants;
- reusing packaging and other materials (paper bags, boxes, plastic tubs, etc.);
- picking up trash.

Another powerful way to model caring for the environment is through gentleness in behavior. People who care are gentle with other living things. They do not break branches on bushes or trees; they avoid picking wildflowers; and they step over or around ants, insects, and caterpillars. Their behavior is based on the maxim "let it be" when it comes to such things as bird nests, ant hills, wildflowers, and habitats under rocks and logs.

## Maintain a warm, accepting, and nurturing atmosphere

Young children learn best in a warm and friendly environment. They need to know that they are valued and that they can trust the adults who work with them. A close, trusting relationship between child and teacher is essential for the child to feel safe and supported in his or her efforts to explore and experiment.

Best practices in early childhood education call for positive connections and relationships (Bredekamp and Copple 1997, Kostelnik *et al.* 2007). These connections and relationships need to be established with adults, peers, and the world of nature. Teachers foster such relationships primarily through modeling respect and caring.

## Focus on the beauty and wonder of nature

Children can learn many different things about natural environments. They can learn about nature as a "resource" to be used; they can learn that air, water, and sunlight are important to living things; and they can learn that elements of the natural world can be grouped into different categories, such as living and nonliving. But the most important thing that young children can learn about the Earth is that it is full of beauty and wonder. It is a sense of wonder that will serve as the strongest incentive to save Planet Earth. It is also a sense of wonder that will add immeasurably to children's enjoyment and appreciation of life.

## Spiritual development

Wonder is one of the manifestations of the spiritual life of young children. While spiritual development isn't often included as one of the developmental domains of childhood, a growing body of evidence indicates that children have spiritual capacities and experiences which shape their lives in powerful and enduring ways (Hart 2005). Recently, discussions about spiritual development are beginning to appear in some early childhood textbooks and other publications (e.g. Gordon and Browne 2004, Wilson 2010b). Because some people may be unsure or uncomfortable about listing spiritual development as a developmental domain, we might use the term "spirituality" and discuss this as an integral dimension of who we are as humans (Tisdell 2001). We might also talk about our need for spiritual meaning and satisfaction, as Kellert (1993) does in discussing the biophilia hypothesis (a theory that we, as humans, have an innate attraction to life and living systems). We depend on nature, Kellert says, to meet our "craving for aesthetic, intellectual, cognitive, and even spiritual meaning and satisfaction" (Kellert 1993: 42). Louv (2006: 34), in calling for a "nature–child reunion," also talks about the spiritual benefits associated with positive connections with nature: "How blessed our children can be – biologically, cognitively, and spiritually – through positive physical connection to nature."

Of course, there are some misconceptions about spirituality. One such misconception is that spirituality is tied to religion (sometimes defined as a belief in and reverence for a supernatural power). Spirituality is actually more aligned with "spirit" than with "belief." Spirit is the vital principle or animating force within living things. Spirituality puts us in touch with this force.

According to Hart (2005), wonder is one of the "spiritual capacities and experiences" of young children and includes such feelings as awe, connection, joy, insight, and a deep sense of reverence and love. Such feelings are often linked to a sense of the sacred and as being integral to spirituality. Such feelings are also associated with deep connections with nature.

While some early researchers and theorists in the field of early childhood education (e.g. Montessori, Froebel, and Steiner) promoted attention to the spiritual life of children, this aspect of child development tends to receive little attention in the professional literature. Additionally, there are strong forces in many communities which work against the spiritual development of children and families. These forces – which include materialism, mechanism, unbridled competition, and individualism – "tend to 'desacralize' the world, leaving it as inert matter for our manipulation" (Hart 2005: 165).

By recognizing, supporting, and honoring children's sense of wonder and their unique way of knowing the world, we can counteract the forces that work against their spiritual development. Of course, we can't teach spirituality, and holistic development isn't something we give to children. Yet, we can support the spiritual life of children and foster their holistic development in a variety of ways. One way is to provide rich opportunities for frequent positive experiences with nature. Such opportunities will foster children's sense of wonder and help them grow in body, mind, emotions, and spirit.

# 6 Fostering academic goals

Knowledge without love will not stick, but if love comes first, knowledge is sure to follow.

(John Burroughs)

The discussion in this chapter focuses on academic goals and how they can be fostered in natural environments. The term "academic" is often associated with traditional subject areas taught in a formal school setting, such as reading, mathematics, science, and social studies. Related goals can include desired learning outcomes in the areas of knowledge, skills, attitudes, and values. The main focus of academic learning, however, tends to be on knowledge and skills – with a great deal of emphasis on the cognitive domain. Academic goals are sometimes differentiated from developmental goals, which are more holistic in nature – emphasizing all the developmental domains (physical, emotional, social, cognitive, etc.).

Some early childhood educators may question the appropriateness of academic goals for children under the age of five. They may ask, "Are academic goals and standards compatible with best practices in early childhood education?" Just asking this question is likely to arouse a strong emotional response from many teachers of young children. It has certainly generated confusion and apprehension in the early childhood community.

Talking about academic goals for young children raises the fear of imposing curriculum on young children that is not appropriate for their level of development and can lead to lasting harm. David Elkind (1987) addressed this concern over twenty years ago in his book, *Miseducation*. According to Elkind, miseducation occurs when educational programs intended for school-age children are appropriated for the education of young children. The dangers of such appropriation, Elkind (1987: xiv) says, include both short- and long-term risks. In the short term, children become stressed; in the long term, they may experience "lifelong emotional disabilities."

Others, too, have raised serious concerns about taking childhood away from children through the too-early introduction of academic studies. In *Reclaiming Childhood*, William Crain (2003) argues for letting children be children in an achievement-oriented society. He calls for a "child-centered" approach to early childhood education – with a curriculum based on the spontaneous interests and feelings of the children themselves. A child-centered approach is based on respect for children's interest in and efforts to learn on their own. Teacher-directed "instruction" generally has no place in this approach. This doesn't mean, however, that we should let go of academic goals for young children. What's needed is an approach that matches young children's way of learning. Early instruction miseducates "not because it attempts to teach, but because it attempts to teach the wrong things at the wrong time" (Elkind 1987: 25). Healthy education, on the other hand, supports and encourages children's spontaneous learning.

It is appropriate to have academic goals for young children. What is sometimes viewed as a dichotomy between an academic curriculum for young children and best practices in early childhood education can be rectified – as long as the academic goals and methods used to accomplish these goals are carefully matched to the developmental and individual characteristics of young children. Carefully selected early learning standards can even be used to provide focus on the academic goals for young children.

Standards – or early learning goals – are statements that describe expectations for teaching and learning. While they can be beneficial in developing curriculum, they can also be misused. There are some educational and developmental risks associated with the use of standards and academic goals if the standards are not well developed and implemented (Gronlund 2006).

Standards and early learning goals have not always been used appropriately and have led to misguided practices in teaching and assessing young children. Such misguided practices are not in the best interests of children and have frustrated many teachers. Many educators feel that "standards-based" education – which includes the concept of accountability – adds an undue layer of stress to their work and takes the fun and spontaneity out of teaching. They also fear that increased attention to standards and academic goals comes at the expense of attention to social skills and emotional well-being (Gronlund 2006).

Yet, it need not be this way. Academic goals and developmentally appropriate practices aren't necessarily at odds with each other. Both can be consistent with best practices in early childhood education. A rich, play-based curriculum can be an appropriate and effective context for implementing the expectations of early learning standards. This chapter will focus on how to do this within a natural outdoor setting.

We don't have to look far to find a listing of early learning standards for the academic areas of literacy, mathematics, science, social studies, and the arts. Various professional organizations and governmental bodies have identified and articulated standards that define what young children should be learning. Early childhood educators are now faced with several related challenges including (1) identifying which academic standards are appropriate for young children, and (2) implementing the standards in developmentally appropriate ways.

The first challenge for early childhood teachers is identifying which academic standards and goals are appropriate for young children. Teachers need to realize that not all published early learning standards are based on the characteristics of young children and how they learn. Young children learn differently from older children – standards and goals for different age groups should reflect these differences.

> Standards for children younger than kindergarten age differ from those for older children because the primary tasks of young children are to acquire and refine foundational skills – skills that will help them successfully learn the content and information of the later grades.
>
> (Gronlund 2006: 3)

Early learning standards should never be strictly academic – that is, limited to traditional content areas associated with schooling. Standards for young children should include social and emotional development, physical development, and approaches to learning. The expectations for children articulated in the standards or early learning goals should be age-appropriate, reflective of cultural differences, and flexible in the rate of acquisition of skills and knowledge (Gronlund 2006).

A second challenge is to implement the standards in developmentally appropriate ways. Skilled early childhood teachers have already been doing this. Even before the term "standards" was introduced to the educational community, teachers were using everyday tasks and routines to help children learn about themselves and the world around them. They were fostering language by talking to the children, developing early literacy by reading and discussing children's books, and promoting understanding of the physical world by providing rich opportunities for children to interact with a variety of hands-on materials (water, sand, logs, grass, etc.) and tools (shovels, rakes, magnifying glasses, etc.).

"Good" early childhood practices, then, do support academic goals. In fact, teachers can look to carefully selected early learning standards and academic goals to make children's play even "more ripe for learning" (Gronlund 2006: 11). According to Gronlund, more purposeful and productive play results when teachers carefully plan the following:

- the setup of the environment;
- the kinds of materials that are available;
- long periods of time for exploration;
- how adults interact with children – i.e. more as facilitators than instructors.

Gronlund (2006) suggests using two different approaches when planning and implementing standards-based curriculum: naturalistic and intentional. With the naturalistic approach, "standards are infused in all that goes on" (Gronlund 2006: 11). This approach requires conscientious attention to what children are doing and familiarity with early learning standards. Using this approach, teachers identify what standards or goals are embedded in what children are doing as they play, explore, and experiment. They then observe and document what children are doing and learning as they play.

The intentional approach is more proactive. With this approach, teachers plan activities and materials that are directly related to specific early learning standards and goals. At times, this may include teacher-initiated activities – but rarely involving direct instruction. Both the naturalistic and intentional approaches add "a layer of awareness" to the planning and implementation of curriculum (Gronlund 2006). This layer of awareness can make activities more interesting to children, enhance the richness of the learning opportunities, and help in articulating and documenting the learning that occurs.

A natural outdoor environment with opportunities for active engagement is ideal for fostering a wide variety of academic goals. Following are some examples of how to capitalize on such opportunities in relation to specific academic goals and early learning standards in the areas of literacy, mathematics, science, social studies, and the arts (specifically art and music). These examples reflect both the naturalistic and intentional approaches to implementing curriculum.

## Literacy

*Academic goal:* Able to follow directions.

*Related early learning standard:* Children listen to and follow through on one- or two-part directions (e.g. "Find your partner and go with them to the strawberry patch.").

This goal can be addressed through a wide variety of teacher-initiated activities as well as child-initiated activities. For teacher-initiated activities, directions should be simple and clearly stated. Children are easily distracted and not always focused on what the teacher is saying. To achieve the academic goal of following directions, children will first need to listen and process what was said.

Teachers can help children focus by alerting them to the fact that they will be giving them directions on what to do. Remind them to listen carefully. Example: "We're going to play by the pond today. Before we go, I need you to listen very carefully. Take your partner's hand and follow me." For some children, it may even be necessary to have them repeat the directions once they've been given. The directions can be repeated back to the teacher or to a peer.

When giving directions to an individual child, it's good to first call that child's name and then wait for his or her full attention. Of course, it's also important for teachers to model good listening by giving full attention to a child who is talking.

Child-initiated activities that promote the ability to follow directions include group dramatic play and construction activities. In dramatic play, children often assign a variety of roles to themselves and to their peers: "You be the lion and growl at me when I walk on the path." In construction activities, children tend to give suggestions and directions as they try to make something work: "Hold this basket while I tie it to the bike."

*Academic goal:* Show interest in books.

*Related early learning standard:* Children listen to children's literature when read aloud.

While many teachers read stories and books every day, they usually do so while indoors. Sharing stories and books in an outdoor setting adds variety and interest. For some stories and books, the outdoor setting can also provide a more meaningful context. Books can be carefully chosen to more closely match the setting – e.g. under a tree when reading about trees, in the garden when reading about sunflowers, etc.

Books can also be selected to help children become more aware of the natural environment in and surrounding the play yard – nonfiction books about rocks, earthworms, and butterflies, for example.

Sharing books outdoors can be done with individuals or groups of children. Sitting in a circle on some soft grass can be pleasant for group story time, but other special "gathering places" might also be used. Sitting on logs, rocks, tree stumps, etc. can be fun. Children may also want to look at books on their own while outdoors. A small child's bench can be an inviting place for a child to look at a book on their own or shared with a friend.

Some teachers hesitate in taking books outdoors as they're concerned about damage to them. Books should be treated with respect, of course, but backpacks, baskets, and wheeled carts work well for transporting books from the indoor to the outdoor setting.

*Academic goal*: Engage in early writing (scribbles, lines and shapes).

*Related early learning standard*: Children use pretend writing during play activities.

Children engaged in pretend writing demonstrate an interest in and understanding of the writing process. Adults can foster this academic goal by providing many opportunities for children to play with a variety of writing tools and materials throughout the day. Such opportunities should not be limited to indoor settings. A variety of dramatic play activities outdoors can encourage early writing – keeping "field notes" or journals, drawing maps, and recording weather changes and plant growth can all be encouraged in a natural setting.

Children may also want to make greeting cards, draw pictures, and write stories during their outdoor play. Child-sized tables should be provided. Clipboards can also be used. Another way to encourage writing in the outdoor setting is to give children materials and ideas for making signs (for labeling, giving directions, demonstrating, etc.).

## Mathematics

*Academic goal*: Matching and categorizing.

*Related early learning standard*: Children demonstrate ability to match and sort objects according to specific attributes (e.g. shape, size, color, etc.).

Teachers encourage matching and categorizing by providing many opportunities for children to work and play with interesting manipulatives. Natural materials – such as stones, shells, pine cones, seeds, twigs, sand, dirt, etc. – make excellent manipulatives. These materials offer a rich variety of textures, colors, shapes, and sizes. Many of them stimulate multiple senses (e.g. sight, feel, scent, etc.) at once. Children tend to show greater interest in natural materials if they collect them on their own versus having the materials collected in advance by the teacher. Collecting on their own also helps children associate the item with its natural context – pine cones and acorns from trees, for example.

Sorting and categorizing can also be encouraged by providing a variety of trays and other containers for displaying the materials. Egg cartons, shoe boxes, divided trays, etc. work well for this. It's best to allow children the opportunity to be creative and self-directed in the way they organize and sort their materials. Young children are often eager to share their ideas for sorting and displaying materials, so a listening ear is always appreciated. Back-and-forth conversation between child and teacher during the sorting process can be interesting and instructive. The extent and direction of the conversation, however, should be left up to the child.

*Academic goal*: Counting.

*Related early learning standard*: Children show interest and curiosity in counting.

Counting is a typical part of everyday life. Young children are soon aware of this and want to try it out on their own. They see adults using numbers when they put candles on a birthday cake, count out napkins or cupcakes, and add two eggs to the pancake mix. While outdoors, children may notice two birds at the bird feeder, five peas in a pod, two empty buckets, etc. These observations should be recognized. Asking children to count, however, should be avoided if its sole purpose is assessment or drill. Children may spontaneously count when adding stones to a pile or "planting" sticks in a row. Whether or not their total matches the actual count doesn't really matter. Children may debate among themselves about the actual number of objects they found or are using, and they may even ask for assistance. This is fine, but insisting on one-to-one correspondence isn't what's important at this point. It's the idea of counting and their interest in quantity that should be noted and encouraged.

*Academic goal*: Spatial awareness.

*Related early learning standard*: Children understand basic concepts relating to location, space, and movement in space.

Loose parts in a natural environment are ideal for helping children learn such concepts as up, down, behind, on, under, near, beside, etc. Play in natural environments can also help them develop spatial awareness as they move their own bodies in space (climbing on logs, standing under a tree, running through a pile of leaves, etc.). As children work and play in the outdoor setting, teachers can unobtrusively provide some commentary (narration) about what the children are doing and experiencing. They can describe – or narrate – a child's action in terms of directionality ("You climbed over the log." "Ramona put the pine cones in a bucket.").

Teachers can also engage children in back-and-forth conversation about what the children are doing. For example, when Tony rolls a log over and notices some "bugs" moving about, the following conversation might take place.

"Do these bugs live under the log?" Tony asks.

"Let's see; maybe we could find out," responds the teacher. "Maybe we could look for tracks or tunnels."

"I see some paths. I think the bugs dig out tracks. That way they can move around under the log," suggests Tony.

"That could be right," responds the teacher. "After we're finished looking, let's be sure to put the log back where it was, because it's a part of the bugs' house."

A number of spatial awareness concepts were included in this brief dialogue. Tony demonstrated an awareness of "under" when he asked about the bugs living under the log. He also demonstrated curiosity about how this would work – that is, how can bugs live and move about under something as heavy and stationary as a log.

The idea of tracks or tunnels was introduced as one possible way to accommodate the movement of the bugs.

*Academic goal*: Measurement.

*Related early learning standard*: Children understand the concept of measurement.

We use different forms of measurement to compare quantities – more or less, bigger or smaller, longer or shorter, heavier or lighter, etc. At times, we use standard references of measurement (yard or meter, pound or kilo, etc.). Other times, we use nonstandard references (width of a hand, length of a shoe, weight of a bucket of sand, etc.). Young children begin showing awareness of measurement when they compare sizes of objects – the big rock and the little stone, for example. Natural materials vary considerably in size and weight. Leaves are a good example. Some leaves are big enough to serve as umbrellas; others small enough to fit inside a thimble.

Frequent opportunities to manipulate natural materials help children grow in their understanding of measurement and ways to compare the sizes of objects. From the broad concept of big and little, they can progress to understanding comparisons with more accuracy (bigger, biggest, longer, heavier, smaller, shorter, shortest, etc.). There are many different ways to foster these understandings:

- converse back and forth with the children as they manipulate objects and compare their sizes;
- model measuring objects one against another – at times using standard measurement tools, at other times using nonstandard references;
- provide a variety of measuring tools (rulers, scales, etc.);
- record the results of measuring on simple graphs and charts, especially of things the children have been actively involved with (growing plants, number of ripe tomatoes, etc.);
- encourage children to figure out ways to record their own results of measurement activities (drawings, sketches, graphs, etc.).

## Science

*Academic goal*: Scientific inquiry.

*Related early learning standard*: Children show curiosity by asking questions and seeking information.

Young children are naturally curious. They tend to ask a lot of "what" and "why" questions and boldly set forth exploring and experimenting. If not thwarted by adults and limited opportunities, young children tend to spontaneously act as scientists without coaching from adults.

Natural environments provide rich opportunities for scientific inquiry. There are so many elements and processes to explore, a wide variety of situations that invite "what if" and "why" questions, and interesting situations encouraging children to figure things out for themselves.

At first, young children will engage in a great deal of trial and error behaviors before they begin to act with intent and purpose. Adults can encourage an understanding of scientific inquiry by engaging in dialogue with the children about what they are observing and experiencing, and ways in which they are using materials. Adults can ask open-ended questions as children explore ("Where do you think this animal lives?" "What do you think would happen if we moved this plant to the sand area?" "What changes do you notice along the path?" "How else could you use this board to help move the rock?"). Adults should also encourage and respond positively to children's questions and comments. It's OK to challenge a child's thinking as long as it's done in a spirit of inquiry and positive support – "Why do you think it's going to rain soon?" "What else could you do to hold that rock in place?"

Adults can also foster scientific inquiry by encouraging children to record or represent what they observe and discover. Children can make drawings of their discoveries and ask adults to record dictated descriptions. Children can also create their own versions of charts and graphs to record their findings.

*Academic goal*: Explore physical properties of materials.

*Related early learning standard*: Children use one or more of their senses to gather information about the physical world.

There are many ways in which the natural world stimulates the senses – gradations of light and color, birdsong, water splashing, texture variations, etc. Young children will be naturally drawn to what they can see, feel, hear, and smell. Teachers can help young children focus on these sensations through such simple activities as matching items of clothing (or parts of clothing) with textures found outdoors. Teachers can also provide paper, trays of paint, and a variety of natural materials (pine cones, leaves, feathers, etc.) for spreading the paint or making prints of the materials.

Children will also enjoy mixing different materials – sand and water, grass and leaves, sticks and stones, etc. The very act of mixing draws children's attention to the physical properties of the items being manipulated.

Gardening with children provides rich opportunities to smell, feel, and taste natural materials. Flowers and a variety of interesting plants also provide visual delights. Teachers should engage children in conversation about what they see, hear, smell, and feel. Children should be encouraged to describe their sensory experiences – not by quizzing them on colors and shapes, but by inviting them to talk about their discoveries and insights.

*Academic goal*: Familiarity with living things.

*Related early learning standard*: Children recognize that living things need a place to live.

Things that move and have a mouth or claws can be frightening to children. Learning about where animals live and what they eat can allay these fears and arouse interest. Watching videos and looking at pictures in a book will never provide the kind of familiarity with animals that actual observation provides. Children who are supported in their observations of ants, earthworms, and birds will soon make the connections between an animal and the need for habitat or a place to live. Close observations also lead to familiarity and minimize the development of unfounded fears.

Observations can be supported by providing magnifying glasses, binoculars, real or pretend cameras, clipboards, drawing materials, sculpting clay, etc. Observations are also supported when adults pay close attention to children's comments and questions and respond positively to them.

Teachers can encourage close observation of birds by maintaining a bird bath and bird feeder. They might also provide short pieces of yarn and small balls of cotton for the children to put out during the nesting season. One teacher brought in a bird's nest that she had salvaged from her backyard during the winter. The wind had blown the empty nest out of a tree. The children were invited to look closely at the nest and make a list of the different kinds of materials that were used to make the nest. The next day, the teacher presented a challenge to the children – could they build a nest like the one they had observed? The teacher had gathered a collection of materials that were on the list the children had generated the day before. The children went to work with great enthusiasm. It didn't take them long to gain a deep appreciation of the skill and "genius" involved in making a nest.

## Social studies

*Academic goal:* Social connections.

*Related early learning standard*: Children work together as a group to accomplish a common goal.

Helping children learn how to make personal contributions to accomplishing a common goal builds their understanding of how to function successfully as a member of a group. While "getting along with others" was discussed in Chapter 5 as a developmental goal, it is also an academic goal for social studies. To help children understand the goal as it relates to social studies, teachers should frequently articulate the idea of community: "If we work together, we can grow lots of flowers for our friends in the nursing home." "When everyone helps, it doesn't take too long to get all the tools in the basket."

Teachers can also foster an understanding of what's involved in healthy social connections by recognizing children for sharing and thoughtfulness in action. Children can be encouraged to do the same – that is, look for examples of positive interactions and share their observations with others. For example: "Leon helped me wash the bird bath. Now the birds have clean water to drink."

*Academic goal*: Basic economic concepts.

*Related early learning standard*: Children understand some of the ways people earn a living.

With a few simple props, children will find ways to role-play a variety of jobs that people do to earn a living. While children may choose any type of job during dramatic play, the natural environment is an ideal setting for role playing such nature-related jobs as working as a park ranger, a wildlife biologist, a gardener, or a farmer. Many children will need extra adult support for jobs that are not familiar to them. This support can come by way of specific job-related props, books and pictures about different jobs, and visits from people in the community.

Inviting community members to come and show children what they do is an excellent way to connect children with the larger community. Community members can also be asked for ideas (and possibly materials) that help children learn about their jobs or professions. One teacher approached a nursery about plans to help children learn about landscaping. The owner of the landscaping business donated bulbs and seedlings and volunteered to work with the children in planting them at their school. In addition to the bulbs and plants, he also brought tools, packets of seeds, and informational posters. He helped the children make drawings about where to plant the bulbs and seedlings and gave them directions on how to take care of them once they were in the ground. After this visit, the children spent a lot of time pretending to be gardeners and landscape designers. They moved "rocks," planted trees, and sketched out a "special place" for flowers, birds, and pumpkins.

*Academic goal*: Geographic awareness.

*Related early learning standard*: Children develop an awareness of location and place.

Simple maps can be used to help young children reflect on the concept of place and relationships within places. It's always good to start with what children are most familiar with – their homes and/or school. A simple layout can be drawn with the children's input about where places are in relation to each other. If doing a layout of the school or center, the building should be drawn first. A very simple line drawing should be used. Locations of doors and windows might be noted. The parking lot and play yard might then be added. Driveways and sidewalks might be drawn. Large trees and other significant landmarks could also be noted. Places within places could be added. These might include the tree house, the garden, the sandbox, etc.

Of course, children should be given opportunities to draw their own maps. They'll need materials and some simple vocabulary (around, next to, on the edge, etc.). They'll also need someone to listen and respond to their descriptions of what they've drawn.

## Art and music

*Academic goal:* Artistic expression.

*Related early learning standard:* Use creative arts as an avenue for self-expression.

Art education should be as highly valued as other areas of academic learning and can be easily integrated with both developmental and academic goals. Developmentally appropriate art activities contribute to young children's social, emotional, cognitive, and physical development. "They help children focus on their emotions and sense impressions and to include people and natural communities" (Belz 2011: 34).

Art activities with young children should focus more on the process than the product. This means focusing more on the materials and the experience than on what is produced. Keep in mind that arts and crafts aren't the same. Art represents a form of self-expression, while a craft involves following a pre-determined pattern or design to make a product. Art versus craft should be the preferred activity with young children. To enhance the experience, art activities with young children should include exploration and experimentation with multisensory materials, including a variety of natural materials.

Sandra Duncan (2010: 12) refers to nature as a "gift to our senses, minds, and hearts" and suggests that nature's greatest gift "is giving children a beautiful and creative perspective of the world." The arts can be used to help children express their unique creative perspectives. Duncan suggests helping children assume the roles of gatherer, observer, and creator as they interact with nature. As gatherers, children collect gifts from nature – simple things like a shiny speckled pebble or a crumbly piece of tree bark. As observers, children take the time to explore their collections and make decisions about how to display them. As creators, children express their feelings and ideas about nature's gifts through such artistic expressions as sculpting, painting, and drawing. Incorporating natural materials in art activities will call attention to the wonders of nature and foster children's appreciation of the aesthetic qualities of the natural world. "The tactile experience of gathering natural materials and manipulating them to create artwork … boosts children's understanding of, and bond with, the environment" (Song 2010: 71).

Combining art with environmental education is sometimes referred to as "eco-art" and has proven effective in promoting "better education for children in several subject areas" (Song 2010: 69). Eco-art is also consistent with several pedagogical positions of environmental education, including direct experience and place-based learning (Song 2010).

*Academic goal*: Music appreciation.

*Related early learning standard*: Participate in music activities.

According to the philosopher Confucius (551–479 BC), "Music produces a kind of pleasure which human nature cannot do without." Children are never too young to enjoy the pleasures of music, and their participation in music activities can foster their creativity and aesthetic development. Children enjoy both listening to and making music. They also enjoy moving to music and using music as a form of self-expression.

Nature can be used in many ways to foster an appreciation of music. Attending to the sounds of nature (produced by rain, wind, insects, birds, etc.) can sharpen listening skills. Using natural materials to make musical instruments encourages an interest in both nature and music, while also fostering creativity. Wind chimes – which can be made with such natural materials as bamboo sticks or shells – add music to an outdoor playspace.

A "music and movement area" is one of the recommended areas for a Nature Explore Classroom. This recommendation is based on the understanding that "music and movement experiences are vital to children's healthy development" and that "outdoor settings provide an ideal place for children to experiment with musical and movement expression" (National Arbor Day Foundation 2007: 16). Nature in a "music and movement area" serves as more than a "setting" for creative expression; it also serves as an inspiration.

## Integrated curriculum

An activity/learning grid relating different types of outdoor activities to some of the academic areas discussed in this chapter is presented in Table 6.1. The purpose of this grid is to call attention to the idea of one activity meeting multiple goals across academic areas. It reinforces the idea of thinking of curriculum at the early childhood level as being integrated versus divided into discrete academic areas.

**Table 6.1** Activity/learning grid

| Outdoor play activity | Supporting materials | Language and literacy | Mathematics | Science | Social studies |
|---|---|---|---|---|---|
| Dramatic play, cooking | Recipe cards<br>Pots and dishes<br>Measuring cups<br>Stirring utensils<br>Plastic tableware<br>Natural materials<br>Water | "Reading" recipes<br>Sharing ideas<br>Giving directions | Counting<br>Measuring<br>Comparing | Observing properties<br>Observing changes | Appreciating different types of food and ways of preparing food |
| Construction | Sticks<br>Sand<br>Tape<br>Cardboard boxes<br>Drawing materials<br>Stones<br>Reference books | Drawing blueprints<br>Studying books<br>Sharing ideas | Measuring<br>Comparing | Making hypotheses<br>Considering "what if"<br>Learning about gravity | Appreciating different jobs |
| Gardening | Child-sized tools | Studying seed catalogues and seed packets<br>Sketching ideas | Counting<br>Comparing | Learning about weather<br>Learning about plants<br>Learning about food | Appreciating different jobs, types of food, and food production |
| Field study | Sketch book<br>Clipboard<br>Drawing/writing materials<br>Guide books<br>Magnifying glasses<br>Boxes or bags for collecting | Studying books<br>Recording observations<br>Making graphs | Counting<br>Measuring<br>Comparing<br>Categorizing<br>Matching | Hypothesizing<br>Scientific inquiry<br>Drawing conclusions<br>Using observation tools<br>Learning about ecosystems | Map making<br>Geographic awareness |

High-quality early childhood programs do not shy away from early learning standards and academic goals (Gronlund 2006). On the contrary, high-quality programs promote academic goals – but do so in a way that matches the characteristics of young children. Teachers of young children remain "ever ready to teach" (Gronlund 2006: 143). Their approach, however, is not based on clearly defined, preplanned instruction and teacher-directed instruction.

Teachers in high-quality early childhood education programs pay close attention to academics and find ways to embed literacy, mathematics, science, social studies, and art and music activities in children's self-selected exploration and purposeful play. What they avoid are "skill-and-drill" activities. They find ways to address academic subjects in an integrated way through playful and exploratory activities. They often use the natural environment as a rich context for fostering academic goals in developmentally appropriate ways.

# 7

# Fostering positive conservation attitudes

A land ethic changes the role of *Homo sapiens* from conqueror of the land-community to plain member and citizen of it.

(Aldo Leopold)

Some may ask how nature play relates to environmental education or the development of an environmental ethic. Others may ask when is it appropriate to tell children that they have a role in "saving the Earth" – when they are eight years old, six, five, even earlier? This question doesn't come with a simple answer. Parents and early childhood educators often struggle with this question and other related issues. They ask: "Should we teach young children about endangered species; is it OK to pick wildflowers and catch insects for close-up study; should young children be involved in cleaning up a community park?"

Many of us want to help children learn about the natural world and feel some urgency in instilling a sense of responsibility for care of the Earth. Yet, we may not be sure about what is appropriate to teach young children and how to go about fostering conservation attitudes or an environmental ethic.

Let's make it clear: "Save the Earth" campaigns are not appropriate during the early childhood years. There are a number of reasons why this is so. While the present state of the environment calls for a great deal of concern, it is not a concern that we should place on the shoulders and in the minds of young children. Placing the burden on children is, in essence, asking them to fix something they did not break and assigning them a task that they are not equipped to handle. Using a "Save the Earth" approach with young children can lead to serious oversimplifications of the issues. It can also lead to feelings of fear and helplessness on the part of children. These feelings work against the development of a positive environmental ethic.

# Fear as a barrier

Fear of the natural world is a part of the "de-naturing of childhood." Too many children are beginning to see nature as our natural enemy. While real dangers do exist in the natural world, the threat is greatly exaggerated (Louv 2006). In fact, many indoor environments are more dangerous to children's health than most outdoor environments. Health-related issues with indoor environments include air pollution, toxic molds, carbon monoxide, radon, lead dust, spread of infectious diseases, toxic cleaning chemicals, hot surfaces, bathtub drownings, child neglect and abuse, choking dangers, falls, etc. A critical review of these health and safety issues gives cause for reconsidering the relative dangers of indoor and outdoor environments.

Fear of the natural environment gets in the way of positive interactions with nature. While there are some things in nature which we have reason to fear (poisonous snakes and spiders, for example), we tend to have unfounded fears of and hold prejudices against other parts of the natural world which pose little or no threats to our safety. Such fears and prejudices may develop in response to cultural messages about the environment.

Some Native American cultures refer to plants and animals as their sisters and brothers. These terms emphasize the positive link between people and other living things. More popular terms used in the dominant culture, however, include "pests," "varmints," and "weeds." We use "bug bombs" and "killer sprays" to rid ourselves of their presence. We read stories about the "big bad wolf" and tell children to stay away from the woods and the water. Our directives to children include: "Don't dig in the dirt – it's messy; don't play in the weeds – you might get hurt; don't touch that shell – it looks slimy; don't go outdoors – it's too cold, or too wet, or too hot, and it will make you sick." If we don't give these messages in words, we may be giving them through our actions. Consider the following statistics published by Serjeant (2006):

- Most people spend at least 95 percent of their time indoors.
- Virtual pets – that can be given food, medicine, discipline, and love – are on the market as an alternative to dealing with live animals.
- Some visitors to national forests have suggested spraying the wilderness areas to get rid of insects and other pests.
- Many people on vacation tend to spend far more time shopping than exploring or enjoying natural areas.
- Large theme parks (such as the Disneyworld theme park in Florida) are among the most popular vacation destinations in the world.

Such messages, attitudes, and behaviors contribute to a serious "psychological detachment" from nature (Slade 1991). They also contribute to a fear of nature. Bixler and his colleagues (Bixler et al. 1994) found fear to be a major deterrent to positive outcomes for urban school children visiting a natural area (a city park). They found that children are often fearful and anxious, and have no idea of what to expect when visiting a natural area. In addition to having a general fear of being in the woods, these children also feared snakes, insects, and spiders. Their list of what they feared included small native mammals (such as squirrels, chipmunks, and rabbits), as well.

Another study (Wilson 1994) focused on the nature-related thoughts and feelings of younger children (ages three through five). In this study, children in a one-on-one setting were asked a set of questions, some paired with pictures of natural settings and/or wildlife. One picture portrayed three baby birds in a nest, with the mother bird feeding them a worm. The children were asked, "What would you do if you were close to these birds?" Responses included more expressions of violence, such as "kill them," "cut their mouths off," "slap 'em," and "kick them," than expressions of care, wonder, or interest. Similar expressions of violence were given when a picture of a monarch butterfly was shown. While what young children say and what they would actually do may not be the same, the expressions of violence are cause for concern. The one-on-one setting suggests that the children weren't copying what someone else had said nor were they trying to impress their peers with outrageous ideas. Their statements were made in a serious, matter-of-fact way.

We can't know with certainty what motivated these expressions of violence. Were the children's statements reflecting the violence they see in the media, or might the expressions of violence be based on fear? One typical response to fear is to fight – "I'll hurt it before it hurts me." But why would children fear baby birds and butterflies? The likely answer is their lack of familiarity with other living things. How many young children have had the opportunity to quietly observe birds and butterflies over time? Children who have little contact with animals in natural environments tend to become fearful of what they don't know.

## Positive experiences with nature

So what happens when children are deprived of positive experiences in the natural world – when their lives are encased in environments devoid of the beauty and complexity of nature? According to Louv (2006), Nabhan and Trimble (1994), and others, the "de-naturing of childhood" leads to some very troubling results including:

- diminished use of the senses;
- attention difficulties;
- higher rates of physical and emotional illnesses; and
- the development of unfounded fears of the natural world.

What does this suggest in terms of teaching environmental ethics at the early childhood level, and should it be done? The answer is a definite "yes" and the reasons for doing so include considerable benefits for both children and the Earth.

Someone has said that "teaching a child not to step on a caterpillar is as important to the child as it is to the caterpillar." This sentiment addresses the developmental benefits of respect for the natural world and a sense of connectedness to it. Environmental psychologists, including Louise Chawla (1990), tell us that positive interactions with the natural environment are important for healthy child development – that children need nature to grow in healthy and holistic ways. They especially need the natural world for some of the "soul-making" aspects of human development, including the appreciation of beauty, mystery, and wonder (Wilson 1996).

While some have referred to this world as a "vale of tears" – a place where we must struggle, work, and suffer – the poet John Keats suggested that we live in a "Vale of Soul-making" – a place that breathes life and a sense of wonder into our beings. Referring to the Earth as "the birthplace of our spirit" – as is sometimes done (Wilson 1996) – is consistent with Keats' sentiment.

Young children seem to be especially responsive to the soul-making aspects of contact with nature. We often see that as young children interact with the world of nature, they experience a sense of wonder, joy, and awe. Nature touches their spirit in deep and profound ways. For young children, nature is seldom just a scene or landscape. They experience it with sheer sensory delight. By helping young children know and relate to the soul-making aspects of the natural world, we connect them to enduring sources of strength, wonder, and joy (Carson 1956). Once children learn to love and respect the Earth, they are likely to care deeply about its well-being. This is the essence of an environmental ethic.

Biophobia (an aversion to nature) is the opposite of biophilia and tends to develop if children's natural attraction to nature is not encouraged or given opportunities to flourish during the early years of life. Biophobia can take a variety of forms and range from discomfort in natural areas to active scorn for whatever is not made or managed by humans. Biophobia is also manifested in the tendency to regard nature as nothing more than resources to be used; and the concepts of "wild" and "wildlife" are viewed in negative ways.

Introducing children to the wonders of nature, then, is as important to the environment as it is to children. As already mentioned, without frequent positive experiences with the natural environment, children are likely to develop fears, phobias, and prejudices against nature. Such attitudes and feelings can become major obstacles to later understandings of and respect for the natural world. There is, in fact, strong evidence suggesting that, to be effective, the development of an environmental ethic must start at the early childhood level, as this is the period of life when basic environmental attitudes and values are established (Elliot 2008).

The early childhood years also represent the first stages in the development of an "ecological self" or "ecological identity" (Elliot 2008, Wilson 2011). One way to describe the "ecological self" is as an individual's connections with and attitudes towards the natural environment (Thomashow 1995). While the ecological self is a part of who we are – and a part of our identity that can expand and mature over time – it often remains unaddressed in discussions relating to child development. With growing concerns about the human/Earth relationship, this may be – and should be – changing.

There's no doubt that the early years mark a period of rapid growth for children in terms of their physical, cognitive, social, emotional, and moral development. We're now beginning to realize that the early years are also a fundamental period for the formation of positive environmental attitudes and a commitment to caring for the Earth. If we factor in the concept of "critical" or "sensitive" periods, we may decide that this issue needs to be addressed with a sense of urgency. Critical periods represent times of heightened susceptibility to acquiring understandings and skills impacting lifelong competencies and attitudes. As early environmental experiences can determine the subsequent development of the ecological self (Elliot 2008,

Wilson 2011), it's imperative that we provide the type of experiences which promote positive conservation attitudes.

## Positive conservation attitudes

Perhaps the most important conservation attitudes to focus on during the early childhood years are empathy, caring, and perspective taking. While the following discussion addresses each of these attitudes separately, considerable overlap exists between them. Some of this overlap relates to differing worldviews – or ways in which we view nature.

For some people, nature is everything in the world that is not human or not made by humans. This view definitely sees humans as separate from nature and may suggest that nature is primarily a resource to be used by humans. Others may equate nature with that which is wild or primitive and refer to it as being undeveloped, unmanaged, or uncontrolled. As these terms suggest, this view focuses on nature more in terms of what it isn't rather than what it is. Helping children develop empathy, caring, and perspective taking in relation to the natural world presupposes a more healthy view of nature – a view that respects the integrity of the natural world and invites a more harmonious human/Earth relationship.

Empathy is the ability to identify with and understand the situation and feelings of others. The "other" can be another person, a group of people, other living things (individually and collectively), as well as living systems, such as ecosystems. Some might suggest that young children are so focused on themselves that they aren't cognitively or emotionally capable of empathy. Research on children's way of knowing the natural world indicates otherwise. Terms such as "primal seeing" and "special affinity" have been used to describe children's unique connections with nature (Sebba 1991, Slade 1991, Pearce 1992). These unique connections allow children to identify with and understand the struggles and needs experienced by other living things.

Adults can support the development of empathy in young children by involving them in the care of living things, by discussing with them what animals and plants need to survive, and by demonstrating gentleness and caring in their interactions with the natural world.

Caring, as a positive conservation attitude, is closely aligned with empathy but also involves a responsiveness to and a sense of responsibility for the other's welfare. Caring is thus clearly rooted in connectedness or relationships, and cannot develop or exist in isolation. Caring is one of those virtues that develops by being "caught" versus "taught."

## Related research

The premise that introducing children to nature during the early childhood years will lead to more environmentally responsible decisions later in life is supported by an impressive body of research. Some of this research has been referred to as "significant life experiences" research. This research is based on the question, "What experiences have led people to commit themselves to working for the environment?" Across different cultures and other areas of diversity, the top two factors leading to a commitment to the environment are (1) frequent positive experiences with nature early in life, and (2) at least one adult who shares the child's interest in the environment. Environmental education at the early childhood level is designed to do both – that is, provide opportunities for children to have frequent positive experiences with nature and to provide adult companionship and guidance in explorations of the out-of-doors. From such experiences, love and care for the world of nature bloom.

There has also been some research on what happens when we inform people about environmental concerns and urge them to live in more environmentally responsible ways. This research indicates that information alone is rarely enough to change people's behaviors towards the environment. Love for the natural world and an appreciation for its beauty and complexity are far more motivating in getting people to take care of the Earth than telling them what needs to be done.

## Community design

Hopes for creating an ecologically sensitive society rest to a great extent on how we educate our children. Fostering a positive environmental ethic at the early childhood level can serve as a critical step in developing an environmentally literate and concerned citizenry. But children need places where they can be immersed in nature that both honor the beauty and integrity of the Earth and provide a safe habitat for children. With this in mind, Moore and Cosco (2006) advocate attention to the following key childhood environmental policy issues:

- Landscape conservation – protect and conserve landscape features with high educational and ecological significance (woodlands, streams, rock outcroppings, mature trees, etc.), especially in areas where childcare centers, schools, and residential neighborhoods are constructed.
- Preservation of special childhood places – places with unusual characteristics are especially attractive to children. These may include both natural places and some people-constructed places (e.g. orchards, old buildings, and other types of structures, such as gates and bridges).
- Livable streets – design features should include sidewalks, trees, other types of vegetation, and measures to minimize and calm traffic.
- Urban wildlife management – places where children play (schoolyards, backyards, and community playgrounds) should include natural features that attract such wildlife as birds, butterflies, toads, snails, and earthworms.
- Rough ground – places where children play (schoolyards, backyards, and community playgrounds) should include natural features that allow children to feel free and interact with nature (e.g. dig in the dirt, manipulate natural materials, pour water, etc.).
- Access to diverse natural landscapes – communities should provide convenient, feasible access to diverse natural landscapes, as effective child development is dependent on richness of experience.

## Place-based learning

One of the pedagogical positions of environmental education involves the concept of place-based learning (Sobel 2004b, Song 2010). This approach emphasizes having children interact with the actual community-based entities they are learning about. This may be the community's social and historical context as well as the larger natural environment. A strong ecological rationale for this approach is based on the idea that we want to take care of that which we know and love. Learning about the place where they live helps children develop a relationship with their own community and a love for their local natural environment. Learning about far-away places is too abstract for children to develop a loving relationship with such places.

Place-based education for young children differs somewhat from that of adults. While adults attend more to the physical and cognitive perceptions of space, children tend to focus on what the space has to offer in terms of activity and meaning. They're interested in what they can do in that space. Children gravitate towards secret and enclosed spaces. Adults may see such spaces as dangerous for children, in that children can't be easily seen or monitored as they play in their special places. "Acknowledging these differing perceptions is fundamental to developing and working with children in a natural outdoor playspace in order to create a sense of place, identity, and belonging" (Elliot 2008: 10).

## Summary

The early childhood years offer tremendous opportunities to foster the child's understanding and appreciation of the environment and to develop a lifelong commitment to caring for the natural world. Connecting children with nature early in life offers the hope of an environmentally concerned citizenry of the future where living in harmony with nature is more of a priority than exhibited by the majority of adults today.

# 8

# Special considerations

No child should grow up unaware of the dawn chorus of the birds in spring. ...
In that dawn chorus one hears the throb of life itself.

(Rachel Carson)

This chapter includes a discussion about three different areas of concern: children
with special needs, technology in the lives of children, and cultural sensitivity. Each of
these areas warrants special consideration in planning nature-related experiences for
young children.

## Children with special needs

For some young children, outdoor time represents the most isolating and intimidating
time of the day. They're unable to engage in the same kind of play activities as most
of the other children in their group – or are uncomfortable doing so. They remain on
the sidelines, observing but not fully participating.

There are a number of reasons why children's enjoyment of and participation
in outdoor activities may be limited. Disabilities, fear, unfamiliarity, and timidity
represent some of the more common reasons. Teachers should be keenly aware of
these and other concerns which may limit the learning potential of outdoor time for
some of the children in their class. Teachers should also be aware of ways in which
they can make outdoor activities accessible to all young children.

Teachers need to realize that not all barriers to full participation in outdoor play
reside within the child. Some barriers relate to the teachers' attitudes and behaviors
and the quality of the outdoor environment. Probably the most important factor in
making the most of outdoor time is the mindset on the part of teachers that "time
outdoors" means more than "recess." The term "recess" implies a break from the usual

teaching and learning activities expected in the classroom and suggests "down time" for both teachers and students. Such a mindset is not conducive to reaping the many benefits of outdoor play and assuring access for all children.

While it's expected that outdoor play will differ in some ways from indoor activities, the rich learning potential of time outdoors deserves special attention. Guidelines presented in the "developmentally appropriate practices" and other early childhood literature accord outdoor time considerable significance (Bredekamp and Copple 1997, Guddemi and Eriksen 1992). The literature indicates, for example, that children tend to engage in different social and cognitive forms of play in indoor and outdoor settings (Frost 1992). According to some studies, boys tend to engage in more dramatic play and longer play episodes during outdoor versus indoor activities (Frost 1992, Quinn 1996).

For most children, outdoor play also tends to be more creative, adventuresome, socially interactive, fun, carefree, and active than indoor play (Frost 1992). Additionally, outdoor play environments – especially those which offer access to natural materials – tend to be rich in sensory stimulation and support a broad range of skills and interests. Such environments support the development of the whole child, including the mental, physical, aesthetic, social, adaptive, emotional, and communication domains (Rivkin 1997, Quinn 1996). Some research indicates that outdoor play also contributes to literacy (Quinn 1996), fosters an appreciation of the natural world, supports the development of naturalistic intelligence (Elliot 2008), and deepens the spiritual life of the young child (Schein 2011).

According to E.O. Wilson's theory of biophilia, people are biologically attracted to nature and need frequent contact with it to find fulfillment (Kellert and Wilson 1993, Quinn 1996). If some children's access to nature is limited, their chances of finding fulfillment through the natural world are also limited.

Both a suitable environment and adult support play critical roles in making outdoor time an enjoyable and valuable learning experience for all young children. Safety and accessibility are two factors that need to be considered in relation to the physical environment and to the role of adults. While these factors are important for all young children, they are even more critical for children with special needs who tend to be at greater risk of accidents, injuries, and isolation than their typically developing peers. Conditions that make them more at risk include problems with balance and motor control, seizure disorders, vision and hearing impairments, hyperactivity, and limited social competence. While adults should be aware of the increased risk for children with special needs, they should not try to create environments or arrange situations that are devoid of opportunities for healthy risk taking. An environment that is free of risk limits children's opportunities for novel experiences. Children need such opportunities to stimulate exploration and, at times, to learn from their mistakes.

There are some guidelines, however, that teachers can use to improve accessibility for children with disabilities. For children with hearing impairments, an adult should remain in the child's field of vision so that it's easier to gain the child's attention, if necessary. For children with visual impairments, tactile markers can be used to define the location of certain equipment and activity areas – sand around a swing area, for example. Sound features can also be added to help orient a child with a visual impairment and make the play environment more interesting. Examples of sound features include wind chimes and bells.

In addition to being free of physical barriers, outdoor environments for young children should also be "psychologically accessible." This means that they should be attractive, secure, and understandable to the children who use the environments (Moore and Wong 1997).

Environments should also be responsive. A responsive environment provides children with immediate feedback when they attempt to interact with elements in their environment. Children tend to lose interest and give up trying when their attempts to control or modify their environments are not successful. Children with disabilities are more likely to have trouble with the responsivity of the environment than their typically developing peers. While a typically developing child may have no trouble turning on the faucet by the outdoor spigot, a child with cerebral palsy may find the task impossible. He or she may try to grasp and move the handle but may not have the motor control and/or strength to accomplish the task. Installing a foot pedal or different type of handle would be one way to increase the responsivity of the faucet.

While early childhood educators generally recognize the value of outdoor play for enhancing the physical development of young children with disabilities, time outdoors tends to be underutilized for fostering social development and the inclusion of children with disabilities. Teacher-mediated activities can be used to facilitate cooperative interactions between children with and without special needs. At times, this may mean adding structure to a play activity. At other times, it may take the form of simplifying a social situation. In teacher-mediated play, teachers generally do not lead or direct the play. Their primary role is to encourage child-to-child interaction. Teachers may suggest activities or the direction of a play situation so as to include a child with special needs. For example, if several children are making "roads" in the sand area, the teacher might suggest that a child with special needs uses some sticks to make a bridge.

Undesignated outdoor playspaces offer considerable advantages over the more traditional playgrounds in providing access for all children. Studies indicate that undesignated playspaces tend to encourage more types of social play, greater frequency of social interaction, language development, more dramatic and constructive play, greater variety of play themes, more object transformations (using one object to represent something else), greater duration and continuity of play, and more problem-solving skills than traditional playgrounds or indoor playspaces do (Frost 1992). Undesignated outdoor playspaces with appropriate play and learning opportunities also lead to less unoccupied and onlooker behavior, as well as less frequent behavior problems than do traditional playgrounds or indoor playspaces (Frost 1992).

Suitable environments in the out-of-doors are perhaps the most ideal environments for learning, in that they foster creativity and exploration and are appealing to children. Research indicates that, unless socialized differently, children love to be outdoors (Quinn 1996). In one research study, when asked to draw their favorite place to play, only four out of ninety-six children depicted inside areas (Moore 1990). Outdoor playspaces, then, if accessible for children with disabilities, offer built-in incentives for children with special needs to interact with materials and people.

Elements of the out-of-doors that make it so appealing to children include association with other living things (plants and animals), immersion in sensory stimulation, opportunities for exploration and hands-on experimentation, and opportunities for more open-ended play. Specific elements of what children like in outdoor environments – as expressed by children themselves – include access to water (especially a waterfall and pond with fish and frogs), flowers that they can pick, a hill to climb on, dens and hiding places, a garden, scarecrows, and very tall and bright flowers (like sunflowers) (Hefferman 1994). Such elements tend to be accessible and interesting to all young children.

Water, as one of the most frequently requested additions to an outdoor playspace, can be added in a variety of ways. Providing buckets, hoses, and sprinkling cans is one easy way to add water if a spigot is available. Water tables – equipped with sponges, paint brushes, cups, etc. – work well, too. Finding a way to have water in motion adds to the fun and the learning potential. Wooden, metal, or plastic troughs might be used for this.

Some design criteria that should be considered to improve accessibility of the outdoor playspace for all children have been outlined by Quinn (1996). These include (1) the use of sensory clues to assist children in experiencing a setting; (2) more space; (3) greater clarity; and (4) plenty of options for use. Greater clarity can be achieved by providing clear definition to the edges of surfaces and activity areas. This, Quinn (1996) notes, can be achieved through changes in types of materials and surfaces. Clarity can also be enhanced by situating major activity areas so that they are clearly visible from playground entrances, by creating surfaced pathways to activity areas, and by defining activity areas with distinct sensory clues such as smells, sounds, textures, and patterns.

In addition to a suitable environment, adult support is also important to making an outdoor playspace accessible to all young children. The role of the adult during outdoor time, however, isn't always understood or appreciated. In response to the question of what she did during outdoor time to foster social development, Lyn, a student teacher in an early childhood special education program, once said, "I work on social development during snack and lunch time. When we're outside, I just let the kids play." Sadly, Lyn seemed completely comfortable with her response. While more experienced teachers may never answer as Lyn did, their behavior sometimes suggests that they hold similar views about what to do during outdoor time. Socializing between teachers, for example, tends to occur frequently during outdoor time. While most teachers recognize the need to supervise young children during outdoor play, their major focus seems to be on safety versus growth and development across the different developmental domains.

While some children will do just fine "on their own" during outdoor play, other children need more modeling, encouragement, physical adaptations, and reinforcement than other children in the group to get the most out of outdoor play activities. While children can, or should, be able to play without being organized or directed by adults, young children often need adults to enable or support play. As expressed by Titman (1992: 5): "Positive play experiences cannot happen in a vacuum however ingenious and creative children may be. Children need time to play, access to environments of quality to play in and other people to play with. They need adults to provide these opportunities."

Following are some specific suggestions as to what adults can do to make outdoor play more accessible and meaningful for all young children:

- Provide a wide variety of play and learning materials so that all children can make choices based on their individual interests, abilities, and level of comfort. A variety of materials for art, dramatic play, and construction (blocks, etc.) can be easily set up outdoors, thus affording a wide variety of choices for children. This is especially important for children who may find large muscle activities difficult or intimidating.

- Provide duplicates of toys to minimize frustration and to encourage social interaction. The sandbox, for example, should have a collection of buckets, shovels, and stirring utensils. There should also be duplicates of riding toys (bikes, wagons, etc.), balls, and dramatic play materials. By reducing frustration, duplicates of interesting materials encourage healthy peer-to-peer interactions and increase safety. A prime cause of bullying on playgrounds is the shortage of materials and the lack of things to do (Rivkin 1995).

- Encourage all children to spend some time engaged in large motor activities. While some children with disabilities or children who are unfamiliar with or fearful of using playground equipment may shy away from climbing, sliding, or swinging, it's important for them to practice skills and develop confidence in what they can do. Teachers should gently encourage them to try new things.

- Don't overprotect children who are timid or who may have disabilities. Overprotection often leads to "learned helplessness" (Wilson 2003b). Teachers should work from the premise that all children are capable individuals who can take an active part in outdoor play. They should keep in mind that goals for the child include independence, skill building, and confidence. When adaptations to the environment are required for children with disabilities, adaptations that benefit all children should be considered, including more space, greater clarity, and plenty of options for use.

- Don't expect all children to engage in outdoor play spontaneously. Some children need modeling, encouragement, and guidance on how to engage in outdoor play. Adults should be available and provide encouragement and support, as needed.

- Encourage peer-to-peer interaction. While outdoors, some children tend to stay close to an adult and may try to keep the adult engaged in conversation or interactive play. The child's behavior may be motivated by the need for protection or attention. An appropriate adult response is to assure the child that he or she will be safe, but that interacting with other children is what is expected.

- Provide opportunities for children to modify their playspaces and play activities by adding loose materials to the play environment. "Loose materials" (such as sticks, stones, cardboard boxes, rug scraps, shells, sorting trays, buckets, etc.) provide excellent materials for creative manipulation of the environment. Through such manipulation, children make a playspace "their own" (van Andel 1990). Such ownership encourages creativity, problem-solving, and more sustained involvement. Thus, rather than developing special places for young children, we should be developing them *with* the children. This means that children's play environments should never be totally finished. By being dynamic and ever-changing, loose parts meet the diverse and changing needs of children during play and promote a wide range of play forms. Children love loose parts. Studies indicate that they are, in fact, "the most popular equipment chosen by children on playgrounds" (Guddemi and Eriksen 1992: 16).

■ Provide "comfort items," such as drinking water, shade, wind breaks and child-sized benches and tables. Consider children's emotional and psychological needs, as well. Be aware that some children prefer small-group versus large-group activities, and offer reassurance and encouragement, as needed. Capitalize on the restorative, healing, and therapeutic qualities of the outdoor environment knowing that they cannot be replicated in an indoor setting (Quinn 1996).

■ Be sensitive to children's feelings and anxieties and be aware that some children fear certain elements of the out-of-doors. It's not unusual for young children to fear bees, spiders, and thunder. They may also fear butterflies and birds. Some children may be fearful of climbing or participating in rough and tumble play. It's often helpful to talk to individual children about their feelings and gradually lead them to a better understanding of what frightens them. Children should also be assured that adults are concerned about their safety and will be nearby to protect them.

■ Provide opportunities for exploration and involvement in natural spaces. Natural spaces allow children to explore and manipulate their environment in a way that doesn't work in more organized or formalized places.

■ Talk with parents and therapists about children's fears, special needs, and interests. For children with disabilities, it's especially important to know which activities and kinds of equipment will benefit each child and which may be too difficult or harmful to them.

■ Adapt the outdoor playspace, as necessary, for children with physical disabilities. Following are several suggestions as to how this might be done:

   – Replace gravel or sand with wood shavings as ground cover. It's easier for a child in a wheelchair or a child with leg braces to move across wood shavings than gravel or sand. Wood shavings are also impact absorbent, making the environment safer if children should fall.

   – Attach straps to swings or use bucket seats to help children with posture and balance difficulties on a swing set. Swings that accommodate wheelchairs might also be used. A fold-up ramp on a platform swing allows wheelchair access. Clamps hold the wheelchair in place as the entire platform swings back and forth.

   – Embed a slide in the side of a hill. Such an arrangement eliminates steps as a barrier to using the slide. It also greatly reduces the risk of injury from a fall.

   – Provide an elevated sandbox and garden area so that children in wheelchairs can have easy access.

All children can benefit from a wide variety of activities outdoors. In addition to fostering large and small muscle development, outdoor play contributes to cognitive, language, social, and emotional skills, as well. Additionally, outdoor play time can provide excellent opportunities for children to interact effectively with others and to develop confidence and self-esteem.

Outdoor playspaces for young children should provide a stimulating, safe, and exciting "place to be." They should be reflective of and responsive to individual children's needs and interests. Providing access to natural areas greatly enhances the play and learning potential of outdoor playspaces, as nature offers sensory stimulation and rich opportunities for exploration and involvement.

Outdoor playspaces for young children should be designed as "special places" – that is, places in which children can experience joy and delight and in which their natural sense of wonder is recognized and encouraged. Outdoor playspaces should also be accessible to all young children, so no child is left on the sidelines as a passive observer.

## Technology in the lives of children

Currently, the role of technology in early childhood education and the parameters on how to use it aren't clearly articulated. As a result, the use of technology in early childhood education remains a controversial topic (Van Scoter *et al.* 2001). Both parents and educators have concerns about possible harmful effects of using computers and other forms of technology with young children. They cite concerns relating to a possible waste of time and money, neglecting more hands-on and sensory activities, keeping children inside too much of the time, and using technology as a solitary versus social experience, thus providing less time for children to interact with others (Cordes and Miller 2000).

Both research and professional opinion in early childhood education, however, attest to the potential benefits of technology for young children's learning and development (Bredekamp and Rosegrant 1994, NAEYC 2012, Wright and Shade 1994). A review of the literature indicates that new technologies are consistent with the principles of learning identified through recent research on brain development (Van Scoter *et al.* 2001). Yet, as expressed in the professional literature, computers and other forms of technology can be misused when working with young children.

Technology – especially computers – has been used successfully to enhance children's social, language, and cognitive skills (Seng 1998). Research indicates that computers can also facilitate social interaction and meaningful conversations with young children (Clements and Natasi 1993). And, as most children (including children with disabilities) tend to find technology (especially computers) intrinsically motivating, its use is supportive of positive attitudes about learning (NAEYC 2012).

While there are many reasons to use technology with young children, there are also some related concerns. One concern has to do with the six and a half hours each day that many children spend using electronic equipment (Zimowsky 2008). This over-reliance on electronic technology reduces the amount of time children engage in physical activity; and this is a serious health concern as physical inactivity is the "primary culprit" of obesity in children (Pica 2006).

Another concern relating to the use of technology with children relates to a possible "rewiring of the brain" (Ritter 2008). Recent research suggests that daily exposure to digital technologies (such as the Internet) "might be changing the way we read, learn, and interact with each other" (Ritter 2008: 1). Some of the possible negative effects of the "rewired brain" include social awkwardness, isolation, the inability to interpret nonverbal messages, and less interest in traditional classroom learning (Ritter, 2008). These effects may be strongest in "digital natives" – that is, those who have been "digitally hard-wired since toddlerhood" (Ritter 2008: 2).

The use of electronic technology can also reduce the amount of time children spend outdoors. For a growing number of child development specialists, this is cause for concern as a close connection between young children and the natural world is important for both the holistic development of the child and for the development of environmental ethics (Louv 2006). Research studies indicate that one of the most effective ways to instill a lifelong sense of caring and responsibility for the natural world is to give young children frequent positive experiences with the world of nature (Chawla and Hart 1995).

Unfortunately, many children today do not have frequent opportunities for exploring the natural world. The result is a "de-naturing of childhood" and the development of symptoms related to "nature-deficit disorder" include attention deficits, depression, and unfounded fear of the natural world (Louv 2006).

Technology is a valuable tool that can be used to enhance young children's learning. When not used appropriately, however, computers and other forms of technology can impede the healthy development of children. This doesn't mean that technology should be removed from early childhood classrooms, as technology does have an important role to play in early childhood education. "The critical factor is a balanced approach to technology in learning, with thoughtful planning to provide for the important needs of childhood" (Van Scoter *et al.* 2001: 1).

The "important needs of childhood" include engaging hands-on activities, close relationships with caring adults, positive interactions with peers, and vigorous physical activities (Van Scoter *et al.* 2001). For holistic development, children also need frequent positive experiences in natural environments.

Becoming familiar with nature and learning to appreciate what is beautiful and wondrous about the natural world should be an integral part of every young child's experience. The best way to learn about nature is to interact with it. Technology, however, can also be used to help children learn about the natural world. It's not a matter, then, of choosing either technology or hands-on exploration of nature to learn about the natural environment and one's place in it. The key is finding the appropriate balance between technology and hands-on experiences in nature so that children (and their teachers) can appreciate each as a path to learning. Studies indicate that using computers along with supporting activities provide greater benefits to learning than either one alone (Van Scoter *et al.* 2001).

Perhaps the wisest thing we can do when it comes to making decisions about technology with young children is to remember that "we cannot live in the wilderness and forget civilization [or] … live in the heat of civilization … without seeking answers or balances in the wilderness" (Lindbergh 1969: vii).

Classrooms today – including classrooms for preschool children – tend to have computers available to the children on a regular basis. Some parents and educators are suggesting that this may not be in the best interests of the children. They argue that computers inhibit creative thinking, movement, human interaction, and attention spans (Richtell 2011). They also argue that computers and other technologies may be a distraction and get in the way of more meaningful learning. When it comes to learning about the environment, this may be especially true. Guidelines for excellence in both environmental education and early childhood education call for experiential, hands-on learning, yet we know that "being wired is a way of life" for many children (Listfield 2011).

Environmental education materials used by many early childhood educators today reflect a lack of clarity on how to use computer software, videos, and other types of technology in concert with hands-on explorations in the out-of-doors. Some teachers rely almost exclusively on some form of print (books) or non-print media (DVDs, computers, etc.) to help children learn about the natural environment. This approach provides limited opportunities for children to develop reverence for life, as it tends to focus on cognitive learning versus emotional attachment. This approach often leads to distorted views of nature and results in many children seeing nature as an abstraction or simply as a resource to be used. Additionally, overdependence on technology can be harmful to young children by diminishing the life of the senses and jeopardizing their social and emotional development. Other teachers provide rich opportunities for children to freely explore the natural environment but fail to take advantage of related resources (including technology) which would extend and deepen children's learning. The key to effective learning is to pair carefully-selected technology with rich hands-on nature-related experiences. As Richard Louv (2011: 5) in *The Nature Principle* notes, "The more high-tech our lives become, the more nature we need to achieve natural balance. ... Utilizing both technology and nature experience will increase our intelligence, creative thinking, and productivity."

## Cultural sensitivity

Article 29 of the United Nations Convention on the Rights of the Child outlines some of the primary goals of education. These goals include:

> the development of respect for the child's parents, his or her own cultural identity, language and values, for the national values of the country in which the child is living, the country from which he or she may originate, and for civilizations different from his or her own.

The anti-bias curriculum – one of the major initiatives in early childhood education, especially in the United States – provides a framework for addressing some of these goals.

While first published over twenty years ago, *Anti-Bias Curriculum: Tools for Empowering Young Children* (Derman-Sparks and ABC Task Force 1989) remains an invaluable resource for guiding our thinking about cultural identity and diversity. An updated edition – *Anti-Bias Education for Young Children and Ourselves* (Derman-Sparks and Olsen Edwards 2010) – provides additional insights on how to help children and families appreciate their own cultural identity and values while respecting peoples and cultures different from their own.

One of the core goals of the anti-bias curriculum includes helping each child "express comfort and joy with human diversity" (Derman-Sparks 2011). For this goal to be realized, adults working with children must also express comfort and joy with human diversity. One way to do this is to incorporate children's home cultures and languages into the daily learning environment and curriculum. At times, this might mean setting aside our own perspectives and preferences to make materials and activities more culturally appropriate to the children and families participating in our programs. For example, to tap into the rich play value of mud, we might plan activities where children use spoons to stir mud, use mud for finger painting, make footprints by walking barefoot through mud, and make mud pies for a pretend party. Some families may find such mud-related activities far outside their comfort zone. The views of these families should be respected and alternative activities planned for children and families not comfortable with mud play. Differing views and values might also come into play if food items (such as cornmeal, rice, corn, cereal, etc.) are used for activities unrelated to snacks or meals, as some families may feel that food should never be used for anything but providing nutrition. To respect these feelings and values, it's best not to use food items for play or for arts and crafts.

Adults should also keep in mind that people's perceptions of what is beautiful or interesting in nature are socially shaped and grounded in culture and familiarity (Duncan 2011). It's important to be sensitive to these cultural differences and respect the attitudes, values, and customs of families and children.

The *Early Childhood Environmental Education Guidelines for Excellence* developed by the North American Association for Environmental Education (NAAEE 2010) call for "culturally appropriate goals, objectives, and practices." Indicators – or what to look for – relating to this guideline include:

- identifying the cultural traditions, perspectives, needs, and interests of the children served and examining the extent to which the program matches these traditions;
- developing staff who have a good understanding of and sympathy with the cultural traditions of the children served;
- involving individuals from the cultural traditions of the children served in planning and pilot testing of programs and materials, and in serving in an advisory capacity on an ongoing basis.

# Epilogue

The concept of considering the "whole" child has been at the forefront of early childhood education for years, but our understanding of what this means is deepening. At one time, teaching to the needs of the whole child meant addressing needs in four developmental domains: physical, social/emotional, cognitive, and communicative (Martin 2011). Today, we know we need to address ecological and spiritual aspects of development, as well. This involves helping children realize that they are a part of something bigger than themselves and that all that exists is in some way interrelated. We're also realizing that for children to reach their full potential, they need to develop empathy and a sense of caring for each other and the natural world.

While self-realization or holistic development has sometimes been referred to as the ultimate goal of education, we now know that "self" doesn't really exist outside its connections with a larger whole. For the self to be fully realized, it must move in concert with the larger whole. Self-realization for any individual can only occur if the process includes a concern for what happens in the larger community (Maslow 1954, Wilson 2011). Education, then, includes a call to strengthen and deepen our own humanity (Mische 2006) and to establish a more peaceful society – a society in which people truly care about each other and all life on Planet Earth.

# Appendix 1: Special places for young children

Several years ago, I visited the outdoor play area of a child care center in a large city. This play area was for young children, one to three years of age. It was approximately thirty-five to forty feet long and only about four feet wide. Its boundaries were defined by the side of a brick building and an iron fence. Children in this playspace could look through the fence and into a parking lot. The surface of the entire play area was concrete covered by a green rubber mat. There were no play materials in this area except a small plastic sandbox and a small plastic slide. I walked into this play area and sat on the green mat, which put me at the eye level of what a three-year-old child might see. I saw the bars of the iron fence surrounding the play area, and I saw a parking lot. There were no trees or bushes; there were no flowers or butterflies. There were, in fact, no living things and nothing to excite my interest or curiosity.

After leaving this playspace for children, I went to a zoo in the same city. I looked at the outdoor areas provided for the animals. The zebras and elephants had trees, bushes, and a pond in their outdoor space. The monkeys had ropes and vines, and the birds had trees and other flowering plants. I saw rich vegetation and interesting structures throughout the zoo grounds. I was pleased for the animals, but wondered about the children at the child care center not far away.

While the outdoor playspace at the child care center may represent the extreme in poor playground design, there are many other early childhood facilities that are greatly lacking in appropriate outdoor environments. Some communities, in response to the need for better outdoor playspaces for children, have constructed elaborate play structures – often made of plastic and representing a type of "magical kingdom." While impressive, such structures are expensive. They also tend to be limited in terms of learning and play potential.

A welcome alternative is the idea of an environmental yard, children's garden, or natural playspace for young children. In the past, playgrounds and gardens claimed their separate spaces and individual agendas. Gardens were designed for beauty and harvest and rarely invited the active engagement of young children. In fact, "don't touch" was most likely the written or unwritten rule when it came to young children. Playgrounds, on the other hand, were designed for physical activity and featured different types of "equipment." The playground design encouraged children to run, jump, swing, and slide but offered little encouragement in other areas of development (e.g. creativity, language, and cooperative play). The traditional playground design is also limited in providing opportunities for developing cognitive understandings in such areas as mathematics, science, social studies, and literacy.

Environmental yards or natural playspaces can take a variety of forms. Some take the form of a children's garden and focus almost entirely on the process of gardening. Such gardens help children learn about the world of nature and the source of our food. Other natural playspaces are designed more for a variety of play and learning activities within a natural setting. Their primary purpose is to provide a safe, nature-oriented play environment that supports and encourages children's growth and development while helping children develop positive connections with the natural world. A well-designed natural playspace offers children the incentives and opportunities to explore and engage in activities that stimulate curiosity and promote independence, spontaneity, and creativity in the physical, cognitive, social, and sensory realms. An added – and important – benefit of environmental yards and playgardens is the nurturing of a love and respect for the world of nature.

Natural playspaces are designed with the characteristics of children in mind – what they're comfortable with, what they like to do, and what they find interesting. Natural playspaces invite children to touch, sniff, be surprised, and find delight. Elements in a natural playspace that seem to have the most appeal to children include tall grasses, trees, a playhouse, a tunnel, water, giant sunflowers, and "loose parts" – such as rocks, sands, and shells – which children manipulate and use for play.

Some natural playspaces include child-size mazes and statues, themes and characters from popular children's books, giant-size models of butterflies, and opportunities for a variety of hands-on activities. Such hands-on activities might include floating leaves or pieces of bark in a shallow stream of water, arranging small stones around a flower bed, digging for worms in a pile of dirt, watering flowers and vegetable plants, rolling down a grassy hill, climbing over bridges, and playing hide-and-seek in a hedge maze.

Environmental yards and playgardens need not be elaborate or expensive to accomplish their primary goals. A tomato plant growing in a broken bucket might be a special garden to a child who has never watched a plant grow to fruition. A row of tulips or zinnias might be a special garden to a group of kindergarten children who grow flowers for their friends in a nearby nursing home. Both provide valuable learning experiences and a sense of joy and accomplishment for children who are involved in the nurturing of these simple gardens.

While the principle of starting simple has great merit, a look at some "remarkable places" for children can also offer insights and inspiration for continued development of natural playspaces for children. The following descriptions of "special places," then, are offered, not as blueprints of what others should strive to develop, but as "idea starters" for what might be added to existing outdoor playspaces for young children.

# Michigan 4-H Children's Garden

Located on the campus of Michigan State University in East Lansing, Michigan, the 4-H Children's Garden offers over fifty theme gardens. There's a Cereal Bowl Garden where rice, oats, and wheat are grown. There's a Pizza Garden where such toppings as tomatoes, onions, peppers, parsley, and basil grow. And there's a Dinosaur Garden where young children discover a topiary stegosaurus surrounded by prehistoric plants. Other gardens are developed around the themes of favorite books, including *Alice in Wonderland* (featuring a maze) and *Jack and the Beanstalk* (featuring giant plants). A virtual tour of the 4-H Children's Garden can be accessed through http://4hgarden. cowplex.com/.

# Rusk Children's PlayGarden

Located at the Howard A. Rusk Institute of Rehabilitation Medicine in New York City, the Rusk Children's PlayGarden was designed specifically to meet the needs of preschool children with varying levels of physical challenges. While landscape architects designed the PlayGarden, they did so with the participation of a team of physical, occupational, and horticultural therapy staff and the teachers from the pediatric unit at Rusk.

The PlayGarden offers a safe space for a full range of motor-planning and physical movement activities. A range of topography, surfaces, and play equipment invites children to run, crawl, climb, bend, jump, and turn. Some of the equipment – specifically, the swings, slides, and ladders – were adapted to allow children with special needs to play easily and safely with others. Gently curving pathways aid in orientation as the children climb over bridges and under arbors.

The PlayGarden also offers rich sensory stimulation. The children can enjoy and learn to discriminate between qualitative aspects of the environment. They can feel the breezes through the grasses and leaves; see the visual patterns and forms presented by such natural elements as flowers and rocks; and explore the differing textures of natural materials such as bark, sand, and water. Other natural elements added to help children experience a full range of sensory stimulation include scented herbs, bright flowers, running water, and wind chimes.

One of the most unique experiences for the children in this beautiful playspace is the ability to interact with rainbows. A prism sculpture, "Over the Rainbow," rotates gently in the wind currents and projects moving rainbows throughout the PlayGarden space. In this "special garden," young children have rich opportunities to explore, to socialize, to rest, and to experience joy.

# Wood Haven Forest School

Four-year-old children at the Wood Haven preschool near Portland, Oregon (USA) spend their entire session (four-plus hours) outside, no matter the weather. Their outdoor classroom consists of several wooded acres bordering on a wetland. Children spend their time observing mallards, beavers, and other wildlife living in the forest. Through active exploration and self-guided inquiry, children learn about

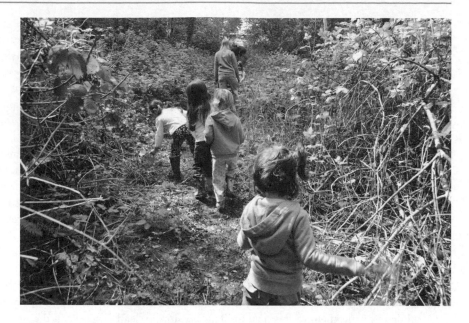

**Photograph A1.1**   Wood Haven Forest School

habitats, seasonal changes, and other natural phenomenon including camouflage, decomposition, and growth cycles of plants and animals. Children also develop confidence and a sense of independence as they learn to interact with different elements of the natural world.

Wood Haven's curriculum is inspired by the principles of Waldorf education and reflects the sense of wonder children experience in the natural world. A flexible routine allows for surprises or "new learning moments" along the way – a planned exploration of sunflowers quickly becomes a study in squirrel behaviour as they come to feast on the seeds (Mann 2011).

Teachers at Wood Haven intentionally foster the development of empathy. One day, this involved building a home for a newt the children discovered. First, the teacher (with the children) imagined what a newt would need and want. After taking a deep breath and filling their lungs with air, they imagined having no lungs. They then tried breathing through their skin. This led to a new interest in and respect for what newts – and other living things – really need to stay alive.

## Schlitz Audubon Nature Preschool

The preschool at the Schlitz Audubon Nature Center (SANC) in Milwaukee, Wisconsin is a fully licensed, nine-month program serving children ages three through five. The SANC has 185 acres of land adjacent to Lake Michigan and includes forests, prairie, and shoreline. The preschool has three different outdoor play areas: the woods, the gardens, and a cabin area. Each of these areas contains many natural elements and "loose parts." The "woods" play area features several trees, logs, long sticks, grass, bare dirt, and a small gully that runs with water when it rains or when snow melts. The "gardens" area has trees, logs, herbs, flowers, vegetables, a wooden play house, a sand area, a compost pile, and a hill with several rocks for climbing. The "cabin" area has a wooden cabin, several trees, sand, grass, and bare ground. Teachers add materials to these different play areas to support imagination and creative play, such as baskets for carrying natural objects, rakes and buckets for leaves, squash and gourds that can be carried, examined, and then observed while decomposing. Children also explore other parts of the 185-acre nature center during daily hikes, varying in time from about thirty minutes to over an hour in duration.

While indoors, children spend most of their time at the different learning centers: dramatic play, books/literacy, manipulatives, building/construction, science, art, and table-top activities. These learning centers feature nature-related concepts and themes and include natural materials. Manipulatives include nature puzzles and animal puppets. Dramatic play props may suggest a camping theme, a farmer's market, or gathering maple sap for sugaring. Examples of table-top activities include making leaf prints, painting a picture of a painted turtle, and planting seeds in a pot that the children made out of newspaper.

The mission of the Schlitz Audubon Nature Preschool is "to provide a high quality early childhood environment that meets preschoolers' developmental needs, while inspiring them to love nature." This mission is clearly evident in the physical environment provided for the young children and the learning materials and activities available to them.

# Appendix 2: Additional resources

## Publications for adults

Adamson, Dawn (2004). *Learning Through Play, the Natural Way*. Langley, BC: Adamson Educational Services.

Berry, Pauline (1991). *Playgrounds that Work: Creating Outdoor Play Environments for Children Birth to Eight Years*. Baulkham Hills, NSW: Pademelon Press.

Bilton, Helen (ed.) (2010). *Learning Outdoors*. London: David Fulton Publishers.

Bilton, Helen (2010). *Outdoor Learning in the Early Years*. London: David Fulton Publishers.

Carlson, Laurie (1995). *Green Thumbs: A Kid's Activity Guide to Indoor and Outdoor Gardening*. Chicago: Chicago Review Press.

Cornell, Joseph (1998). *Sharing Nature with Children*. Nevada City, CA: Dawn.

Curtis, Deb and Carter, Margie (2003). *Designs for Living and Learning*. St Paul, MN: Redleaf Press.

Danks, Fiona and Schofield, Jo (2006). *Nature's Playground: Activities, Crafts and Games to Encourage Your Child to Enjoy the Great Outdoors*. London: Frances Lincoln.

Dannenmaier, Molly (1998). *A Child's Garden*. New York: Simon & Schuster.

Deviney, J., Duncan, S., Harris, S., Rody, M.A. and Rosenberry, L. (2010). *Inspiring Spaces for Young Children*. Silver Spring, MD: Gryphon House.

Deviney, J., Duncan, S., Harris, S., Rody, M.A. and Rosenberry, L. (2010). *Rating Observation Scale for Inspiring Environments*. Silver Spring, MD: Gryphon House.

Elliot, Sue (ed.) (2008). *The Outdoor Playspace Naturally*. Baulkham Hills, NSW: Pademelon Press.

Frost, Joe and Wortham, Sue (eds) (1990). *Playgrounds for Young Children, National Survey and Perspectives*. Available online at http://www.eric.ed.gov/PDFS/ED326492.pdf

Garret, Linda and Thomas, Hannah (2006). *Small Wonders: Nature Education for Young Children*. Quechee, VT: Vermont Institute of Natural Science.

Grant, Tim and Littlejohn, Gail (eds) (2001). *Greening School Grounds: Creating Habitats for Learning*. Gabriola Island, BC: New Society Publishers.

Greenman, J. (2005). *Caring Spaces, Learning Places*. Redmond, WA: Exchange Press.

Johnson, Julie M. (2000). *Design for Learning: Values, Qualities and Processes of Enriching School Landscapes*. Washington, DC: American Society of Landscape Architects.

Keeler, Rusty (2000). *Soundscape Recipe Book*. Ithaca, NY: Planet Earth Playscapes.

Keeler, Rusty (2008). *Natural Playscapes*. Redmond, WA: Exchange Press.

Lovejoy, Sharon (1999). *Roots, Shoots, Buckets and Boots: Gardening Together with Children*. New York: Workman Publishing Company.

Moore, Robin C. (1993). *Plants for Play: A Plant Selection Guide for Children's Outdoor Environments*. Berkeley, CA: MIG Communications.

Moore, Robin, C. and Wong, Herbert (1997). *Natural Learning*. Berkeley, CA: MIG Communications.

Moore, Robin C., Goltsman, Susan and Iacofano, Daniel (eds) (1992). *Play for All Guidelines: Planning, Designing, and Management of Outdoor Play Settings for All Children*. Berkeley, CA: MIG Communications.

NAAEE (2010). *Early Childhood Environmental Education Programs: Guidelines for Excellence*. NAAEE: Washington, DC.

National Arbor Day Foundation (2007). *Learning with Nature Idea Book*. Lincoln, NE: National Arbor Day Foundation.

*PlayRights Journal*. International Play Association (www.ipaworld.org).

Rhoades, Diane (1995). *Garden Crafts for Kids: 50 Great Reasons to Get Your Hands Dirty*. Asheville, NC: Lark Books.

Rivkin, Mary (1995). *The Great Outdoors*. Washington, DC: NAEYC.

Starbuck, Sara, Olthof, Marla, and Midden, Karen (1992). *Hollyhocks and Honeybees: Garden Projects for Young Children*. St Paul, MN: Redleaf Press.

Stetson, Emily and Cole-Stone, J.S. (2004). *Kids' Easy-to-Create Wildlife Habitats: For Small Spaces in City-Suburbs-Countryside*. Carmel, NY: Williamson Books.

Tai, Lolly, Haque, Mary, McLellan, Gina, and Knight, Erin (2006). *Designing Outdoor Environments for Children*. New York: McGraw-Hill.

Titman, Wendy. (1994). *Special Places, Special People: The Hidden Curriculum of School Grounds*. Crediton: Southgate Publishers.

Young, Jon, McGown, Evan, and Ellen Hass (2010). *Coyote's Guide to Connecting with Nature*. Shelton, WA: Owlink Media.

## Children's books about gardening

Burke-Weiner, K. (1992). *The Maybe Garden*. Hillsboro, OR: Beyond Words Publications.

Caseley, J. (1990). *Grandpa's Garden Lunch*. New York: Greenwillow.

Ehlert, L. (1992). *Planting a Rainbow*. San Diego, CA: Voyager Books.

Ehlert, L. (1996). *Growing Vegetable Soup*. Northborough, MA: Sundance Publications.

Florian, D. (1996). *Vegetable Garden*. San Diego, CA: Voyager Books.

Greenstein, E. (1996). *Mrs. Rose's Garden*. New York: Simon & Schuster Children's Publications.

Kraus, R. (1993). *The Carrot Seed*. New York: Harper Festival.

Lobel, A. (1996). *Alison's Zinnia*. New York: HarperTrophy.

Lopez de Mariscal, B. (2001). *The Harvest Birds*. San Francisco, CA: Children's Book Press.

Robbins, G. (1993). *From Seed to Plant*. New York: Holiday House.

Robbins, K. (1990). *A Flower Grows*. New York: Dial.

Rylant, C. (1987). *This Year's Garden*. New York: Aladdin.

Schories, P. (1996). *Over Under in the Garden*. New York: Farrar, Straus and Giroux.

Seymour, P. (1988). *How Animals and Plants Grow*. Cambridge: Lutterworth Press.

# Organizations and other internet resources

Australian Association for Environmental Education (www.aaee.org.au) – includes a national early childhood special interest group.

Children and Nature Network (www.cnaturenet.org) – an international network focusing on the sharing of research, resources, and initiatives about connecting children with nature.

Gardening with Kids (www.kidsgardening.org) – offers suggested children's gardening activities and related resources, including child-size gardening tools.

International Play Association (www.ipaworld.org) – offers resources and information on its international work to promote the child's right to play; an interdisciplinary organization embracing membership of all professions working for or with children.

Learning Through Landscapes (www.ltl.org.uk) – provides training, resources, and support to advance improved use, design, and management of school grounds.

Let's Play Projects (http://letsplay.buffalo.edu/) – focuses on making play accessible for children with disabilities.

National Association for Environmental Education (UK) (www.naee.org.uk) – supports the teaching of environmental education in nurseries, schools, and other educational institutions.

National Wildlife Federation (www.nwf.org) – includes a "Schoolyard Habitats" program and offers materials, suggestions, and guidelines, including a "How-To Guide" for establishing a wildlife habitat in the schoolyard.

The Natural Learning Initiative (www.naturalearning.org) – a research and extension program of the University of North Carolina offering resources and project ideas for outdoor play areas.

Nature Action Collaborative for Children (www.worldforumfoundation.org) – worldwide effort to make nature education a part of the lives of children.

Nature Explore (www.arborday.org/explore/) – a research-based project providing educators, designers, and families with comprehensive resources to connect children with the natural world on a daily basis; offers workshops, publications, and outdoor classroom design consultation.

North American Association for Environmental Education (http://www.naaee.net/) – offers conferences, special interest groups, publications, and other resources for all levels of environmental education.

Planet Earth Playscapes (www.earthplay.net) – offers an array of resources and links for planning early childhood environments, with a special focus on environmentally friendly materials and sensory-rich natural playgrounds.

Project Learning Tree (www.plt.org) – offers workshop and resources focusing on hands-on experiences with trees and nature.

Roots and Shoots (www.rootsandshoots.org) – offers resources to help children become nurturing and caring in their relationship with living things.

Sensory Trust (http://www.sensorytrust.org.uk) – offers resources and ideas on how to make environments more inclusive for persons with disabilities; includes ideas on inclusive play.

Royal Horticultural Society (www.rhs.org.uk) – offers demonstration gardens and a wealth of resources and inspiration for gardening activities for children.

# Program evaluation index

Box A2.1 contains an index or checklist for evaluating an early childhood education program in relation to the major principles outlined in this book.

---

**Box A2.1** Nurturing Nature and Young Children Index

Directions: Use the scale of 1–5 for each item to evaluate an early childhood program in relation to the principles and guidelines presented in *Nature and Young Children* (1 = not evident; 5 = clearly evident).

1. Nature play is an integral part of the daily program.

    1    2    3    4    5

2. The outdoor playspace features a variety of natural elements with hands-on opportunities to interact with natural materials.

    1    2    3    4    5

3. The indoor environment includes a variety of natural materials arranged to enhance the beauty of the room and to invite active exploration on the part of the children.

    1    2    3    4    5

4. Adults arrange the environment and plan activities based on the children's interests.

    1    2    3    4    5

5. Adults demonstrate warmth, respect, and caring in their interactions with children.

    1    2    3    4    5

6. All areas of child development – including spirituality, creativity, and a sense of wonder – are supported.

    1    2    3    4    5

7. Academic goals are fostered through a developmentally appropriate and integrated approach.

    1    2    3    4    5

8. Positive conservation attitudes are promoted through frequent positive interactions with nature, modeling on the part of adults, and opportunities to care for living things.

   1   2   3   4   5

9. The environment and activities are accessible to children with special needs.

   1   2   3   4   5

10. Technology is used selectively and is carefully balanced with a variety of engaging hands-on experiences which include nature play, positive peer interactions, and vigorous physical activities.

    1   2   3   4   5

11. The cultural traditions, perspectives, needs, and interests of children and families are identified and respected.

    1   2   3   4   5

12. Connecting children with nature is one of the major unifying themes evident in the environment, curriculum, and adult interactions with children and families.

    1   2   3   4   5

# References

Basile, C. and White, C. (2000). Respecting living things: environmental literacy for young children. *Early Childhood Education Journal 28*(1), 57–61.

Baylor, B. and Parnall, P. (1978). *The Other Way to Listen*. New York: Charles Scribner's Sons.

Baylor, B. and Parnall, P. (1987). *The Desert is Theirs*. Fort Worth, TX: Aladdin.

Belz, P. (2011). Using art to teach children about themselves and the world. *Exchange 33*(3), 34–6.

Bilton, H. (2002). *Outdoor Play in the Early Years*. London: David Fulton Publishers.

Bilton, H. (ed.) (2010a). *Learning Outdoors*. New York: Routledge.

Bilton, H. (2010b). *Outdoor Learning in the Early Years*. 3rd edn. New York: Routledge.

Bixler, R.D., Carlisle, C.L., Hammitt, W.E. and Floyd, M.F. (1994). Observed fears and discomforts among urban students on field trips to wildland areas. *Journal of Environmental Education 26*(12), 24–33.

Bohling-Phillippi, V. (2006). The power of nature to help children heal. *Exchange 17*(1), 49–52.

Bredekamp, S. and Copple, C. (1997). *Developmentally Appropriate Practice in Early Childhood Programs Serving Children From Birth Through Age 8*. 2nd edn. Washington, DC: NAEYC.

Bredekamp, S. and Rosegrant, T. (1994). Learning and teaching with technology. In J.L. Wright and D.D. Shade, *Young Children: Active Learners in a Technological Age* (pp. 53–61). Washington, DC: NAEYC.

Carson, R. (1956). *The Sense of Wonder*. New York: Harper & Row.

Ceppi, G. and Zini, M. (1998). *Children, Spaces, Relations: Metaproject for an Environment for Young Children*. Cavriago: Reggio Children.

Chawla, L. (1990). Ecstatic places. *Children's Environments Quarterly 7*(4), 18–23.

Chawla, L. and Hart, R.A. (1995). The roots of environmental concern. *The NAMTA Journal 20*(1), 148–57.

Clements, D.H. and Nastasi, B.K. (1993). Electronic media and early childhood education. In B. Spodek (ed.), *Handbook of Research on the Education of Young Children* (pp. 251–75). New York: Macmillan.

Cobb, E. (1977). *The Ecology of Imagination in Childhood*. New York: Columbia University Press.

Cohen, R. and Tunick (eds) (1997). *Snail Trails and Tadpole Tails*. St Paul, MN: Redleaf Press.

Coles, R. (1997). *The Moral Intelligence of Children: How to Raise a Moral Child*. New York: Random House.

Copple, C. and Bredekamp, S. (eds) (2009). *Developmentally Appropriate Practice in Early Childhood Programs*. 3rd edn. Washington, DC: NAEYC.

Cordes, C. and Miller, E. (eds) (2000). *Fool's Gold: A Critical Look at Computers in Childhood*. College Park, MD: Alliance for Childhood. Available online at http://drupal6.alliance forchildhood.org/fools_gold (accessed 21 December 2008).

Cosco, N. and Moore, R. (2006). Playing in place: why the physical environment is important in playwork. Available online at http://www.naturalearning.org/sites/default/files/MooreCoscoTherapeuticGardenLATIS.pdf (accessed 13 March 2012).

Crain, W. (2003). *Reclaiming Childhood*. New York: Henry Holt and Company.

Curtis, D. (2010). *Risk. The Wisdom of Nature*. Ulster Park, NY: Community Playthings.

Curtis, D. and Carter, M. (2003). *Designs for Living and Learning: Transforming Early Childhood Environments*. St Paul, MN: Redleaf Press.

Denham, S.A. (2001). Dealing with feelings: foundations and consequences of young children's emotional competence. *Early Education and Development 12*(1), 5–9.

Derman-Sparks, L. (2011). Antibias education: reflections. *Exchange 33*(4), 55–8.

Derman-Sparks, L. and ABC Task Force (1989). *Antibias Curriculum: Tools for Empowering Young Children*. Washington, DC: NAEYC.

Derman-Sparks, L. and Olsen Edwards, J. (2010). *Antibias Education for Ourselves and Others*. Washington, DC: NAEYC.

Deviney, J., Duncan, S., Harris, S., Rody, M.A. and Rosenberry, L. (2010a). *Inspiring Spaces for Young Children*. Silver Spring, MD: Gryphon House.

Deviney, J., Duncan, S., Harris, S., Rody, M.A. and Rosenberry, L. (2010b). *Rating Observation Scale for Inspiring Environments*. Silver Spring, MD: Gryphon House.

Dimensions Educational Research Foundation (2011). *Growing with Nature*. Lincoln, NE: Dimensions Foundation.

Duncan. S. (2010). Gift of nature. *The Wisdom of Nature*. Ulster Park, NY: Community Products. Available online at http://www.communityplaythings.com/resources/articles/wisdomofnature/Wisdom_of_Nature.pdf#xml=http://192.168.2.11/texis/search/pdfhi.txt?query=the+wisdom+of+nature&pr=Community+PlaythingsUS&prox=page&rord er=500&rprox=750&rdfreq=500&rwfreq=750&rlead=0&rdepth=0&sufs=2&order=r& cq=&id=4f5d91cc7 (accessed 13 March 2012).

Duncan, S. (2011). Breaking the code. *Exchange 33*(4), 13–17.

Elkind, D. (1987). *Miseducation*. New York: Knopf.

Elliott, S. (ed.) (2008). *The Outdoor Playspace Naturally for Children Birth to Five Years*. Castle Hill, NSW: Pademelon Press.

Erickson, D.M. and Ernst, J.A. (2011). The real benefits of nature play every day. *Exchange 33*(4), 97–9.

Finch, K. (2005). Nature-focused preschools. *Interpreter* (July/August). Available online at http://www.greenheartsinc.org/uploads/Copy_of_NAI_article_for_website_new.pdf (accessed 8 October 2011).

Frost, J.L. (1992). Reflections on research and practice in outdoor play environments. *Dimensions of Early Childhood*, Summer, 6–10.

Gardner, H. (1999). *Intelligence Reframed. Multiple Intelligences for the 21st Century*. New York: Basic Books.

Garner, P.W. and Estep, K.M. (2001). Emotional competence, emotion socialization, and young children's peer-related social competence. *Early Education and Development 12*(1), 29–46.

Gill, T. (2007). *Growing Up in a Risk Adverse Society*. London: Calouste Gulbenkian Foundation.

Glaser, L. (1994). *Wonderful Worms*. Minneapolis, MN: Millbrook Press.

Gordon, A.M. and Browne, K.W. (2004). *Beginnings and Beyond: Foundations in Early Childhood Education*. Clifton Park, NY: Delmar Cengage Learning.

Grant, T. (1998). Why environmental education is GOOD education. *Green Teacher*, 56. Reprinted in *Global, Environmental and Outdoor Education Council Newsletter*. Available online at http://www.geoec.org/resources/envedu-goodedu.html#closing (accessed 8 October 2011).

Greenman, J. (1988). *Caring Spaces, Learning Places*. Redmond, WA: Exchange Press, Inc.

Greenman, J. (2005). *Caring Spaces, Learning Places*. 2nd edn. Redmond, WA: Exchange Press, Inc.

Gronlund, G. (2006). *Make Early Learning Standards Come Alive*. St Paul, MN: Redleaf Press.

Guddemi, M. and Eriksen, A. (1992). Designing outdoor learning environments for and with children. *Dimensions of Early Childhood*, Summer, 15–18, 23–4, 40.

Harlan, J.D. (1992). *Science Experiences for the Early Childhood Years*. New York: Macmillan.

Hart, T. (2005). Spiritual experiences and capacities of children and youth. In E.C. Rhehlkepartain, P.E. King, L. Wagener and P.L. Benson (eds), *The Handbook of Spiritual Development in Childhood and Adolescence* (pp. 163–78). Thousand Oaks, CA: Sage Publications.

Hefferman, M. (1994). The children's garden project at River Farm. *Children's Environments* *11*(3), 221–31.

Hines, S. (2005). Go out and play. *Landscape Architecture*, March, 128–36.

Hodgkins, F. (2007). *If You Were My Baby*, Nevada City, CA: Dawn Publications.

Kaplan, R. and Kaplan, S. (1989). *The Experience of Nature*. New York: Cambridge University Press.

Kellert, S.R. (1993). The biological basis for human values of nature. In S.R. Kellert and E.O. Wilson (eds), *Biophilia Hypothesis* (pp. 42–69). Washington, DC: Island Press.

Kellert, S.R. and Wilson, E.O. (1993). *The Biophilia Hypothesis*. Washington, DC: Island Press.

Klein, A.S. (2011). Different approaches to teaching: comparing three preschool programs. *Early Childhood News*. Available online at http://www.earlychildhoodnews.com/earlychildhood/article_view.aspx?ArticleID=367 (accessed 14 July 2011).

Knight, S. (2009). *Forest Schools and Outdoor Learning in the Early Years*. London: Sage Publications.

Kostelnik, M.J., Soderman, A.K. and Whiren, A.P. (2007). *Developmentally Appropriate Curriculum*. Upper Saddle River, NJ: Pearson/Prentice Hall.

Kramer, D. (1992). *Animals in the Classroom*. Menlo Park, CA: Addison-Wesley.

Leopold, A. (1986). *Sand County Almanac*. Original publication, 1949. New York: Ballantine Books.

Lieberman, G.A. and Hooty, L.L. (1998). *Closing the Achievement Gap*. San Diego, CA: State Education and Environment Roundtable. Available online at http://www.seer.org/extras/execsum.pdf (accessed 17 November 2001).

Lindbergh, A.M. (1969). *Earth Shine*. New York: Harcourt, Brace & World, Inc.

Listfield, E. (2011). Generation wired. *Parade*, 9 October. Available online at http://www.parade.com/health/2011/10/generation-wired.html (accessed 8 November 2011).

Louv, R. (2006). *The Last Child in the Woods*. Chapel Hill, NC: Algonquin Books.

Louv, R. (2011). *The Nature Principle*. Chapel Hill, NC: Algonquin Books.

McCloskey, R. (1941). *Make Way for Ducklings*. New York: Viking/Penguin Books.

Mann, H. (2011). Personal communication. Wood Haven. Email, 20 September 2011.

Martin. J. (2011). The whole child. *Exchange 33*(4), 86.

Maslow, A.H. (1954). *Motivation and Personality*. New York: Harper.

Mazer, A. (1994). *The Salamander Room*. Lake Benton, MN: Dragonfly Books.

Miller, D.L., Tichota, K. and White, J. (2009). *Young Children Learn Through Play in a Nature Explore Classroom*. Lincoln, NE: Dimensions Educational Research Foundation. Available online at http://www.dimensionsfoundation.org/research/documents/authenticplay.pdf (accessed 17 November 2011).

Mische, P.M. (2006). Educating for peace and planetary community at the level of our deep humanity. *Global Education Associates, Breakthrough New*, October–December, 5–9.

Mische, P. and Harris, I. (2008). Environmental peacemaking, peacekeeping, and peacebuilding. In M. Bajaj (ed.), *Encyclopedia of Peace Education*. New York: Columbia University.

Montessori, M. (1972). *The Secret of Childhood* (M.J. Costelloe, trans.). New York: Ballantine.

Moore, R. (1990). *Childhood's Domain: Play and Place in Child Development.* Berkeley, CA: MIG Communications.

Moore, R. and Cosco, N.G. (2006). Developing an earth-bound culture through design of childhood habitats. Paper presented at the International Conference on People, Land and Sustainability, University of Nottingham, September 13–16, 2000. Available online at http://www.naturalearning.org/sites/default/files/EarthboundChildren.pdf (accessed 15 November 2006).

Moore, R. and Wong, H. (1997). *Natural Learning.* Berkeley, CA: Mig Communications.

NAAEE (2010). *Early Childhood Environmental Education Programs: Guidelines for Excellence.* Washington, DC: NAAEE.

Nabhan, G.P. and Trimble, S. (1994). *The Geography of Childhood.* Boston, MA: Beacon Press.

NAEYC (2012). Technology and young children – ages 3 through 8. Available online at http://www.naeyc.org/files/naeyc/file/positions/PS_technology_WEB2.pdf (accessed 13 March 2012).

National Arbor Day Foundation (2007). *Learning with Nature Idea Book.* Lincoln, NE: National Arbor Day Foundation.

Nicolson, S. and Shipstead, S.G. (2002). *Through the Looking Glass.* Columbus, OH: Merrill Prentice Hall.

Orr, D.W. (2004). *Earth in Mind.* Washington, DC: Island Press.

Peace Child International (1992). *Children's State of the Planet Handbook.* Amsterdam: Peace Child International.

Pearce, J.S. (1992). *Magical Child: Rediscovering Nature's Plan for our Children.* New York: E.P. Dutton.

Pica, R. (2006). Physical fitness and the early childhood curriculum. *Young Children,* May, 12–19.

Quinn, M.D. (1996). The development and application of design criteria for outdoor play environments for child care centers in Iowa. Unpublished master's thesis, Iowa State University.

Richtell, M. (2011). A Silicon Valley school that doesn't compute. *New York Times,* 22/10/11. Available online at http://www.nytimes.com/2011/10/23/technology/at-waldorf-school-in-silicon-valley-technology-can-wait.html (accessed 8 November 2011).

Ritter, M. (2008). Scientists ask: does the Web rewire the brain? *The Olympian,* 4 December, 1–2.

Rivkin, M. (1995). *The Great Outdoors: Restoring Children's Right to Play Outside.* Washington, DC: National Association for the Education of Young Children.

Rivkin, M. (1997). The schoolyard habitat movement: what it is and why children need it. *Early Childhood Education Journal 25*(1), 61–6.

Roffey, S. and O'Reirdan, T. (2001). *Young Children and Classroom Behaviour.* London: David Fulton Publishers.

Royal National Institute of the Blind (n.d.). London. Online. Available www.rnib.org (accessed 24 November 2006).

Rud, A.G. and Beck, A.M. (2000). Kids and critters in class together. *Phi Delta Kappan 82*(4), 313–15.

Schein, D.L. (2011). A social constructivist grounded theory on spiritual development beginning at birth. Unpublished doctoral thesis, Walden University.

Sebba, R. (1991). The landscapes of childhood: the reflection of childhood's environment in adult memories and in children's attitudes. *Environment and Behavior 23*(4), 395–422.

Seng, S. (1998). Enhanced learning: computers and early childhood education. Paper presented at the Educational Research Association Conference, Singapore, November. (ERIC Document Reproduction Service No. ED 431 524).

Serjeant, J. (2006). "Rejuvenile" adults: healthful, silly or just a bit desperate? *Seattle Times,* 7, August.

Shields, A., Dickstein, S., Seifer, R., Giusti, L., Magee, K.D. and Spritz, B. (2001). Emotional competence and early school adjustment: a study of preschoolers at risk. *Early Education and Development 12*(1), 73–90.

Slade, A. (1991). A developmental sequence for the ecological self. Unpublished master's thesis, University of Montana.

Sobel, D. (2004a). *Beyond Ecophobia: Reclaiming the Heart in Nature Education*. Great Barrington, MA: The Orion Society and The Myrin Institute.

Sobel, D. (2004b). *Place-based Education*. Great Barrington, MA: Orion Society.

Song, Y.I.K. (2010). The earth is our canvas: creating eco-art with children. In J.L. Hoot and J. Szente (eds), *The Earth is Our Home* (pp. 69–91). Washington, DC: Association for Childhood Education International.

Stephens, K. (2009). Imaginative play during childhood: required for reaching full potential. *Exchange*, March/April, 53–6.

Tanner, T. (1980). Significant life experiences: a new research area in environmental education. *Journal of Environmental Education 11*(4), 20–4.

Theemes, T. (1999). *Let's Go Outside! Designing the Early Childhood Playground*. Ypsilanti, MI: High/Scope Press.

Thomashow, M. (1995). *Ecological Identity*. Cambridge, MA: MIT Press.

Tisdell, E. (2001). Spirituality in adult and higher education. (Contract No. ED-99-CO-0013). Washington, DC: US Department of Education. (ERIC Document Reproduction Service No. ED459370).

Titman, W. (1992). *Play, Playtime and Playgrounds*. Crediton: Southgate Publishers.

van Andel, J. (1990). Places children like, dislike, and fear. *Children's Environments Quarterly 7*(4), 24–31.

Van Matre, S. (1990). *Earth Education: A New Beginning*. Warrenville, IL: The Institute for Earth Education.

Van Scoter, J., Ellis, D. and Railsback, J. (2001). Technology in early childhood education: finding the balance. Available online at http://www.eric.ed.gov/PDFS/ED458008.pdf (accessed 13 March 2012).

Wellhousen, K. (2002). *Outdoor Play, Every Day: Innovative Play Concepts for Early Childhood*. Albany, NY: Delmar.

Wilson, E.O. (1984). *Biophilia: The Human Bond with Other Species*. Cambridge, MA: Harvard University Press.

Wilson, R.A. (1994). Preschool children's perspectives on the environment. North American Association for Environmental Education Conference Proceedings, Troy, OH: North American Association for Environmental Education.

Wilson, R.A. (1996). The Earth – a "vale of soul making." *Early Childhood Education Journal 23*(3), 169–71.

Wilson, R.A. (2003a). Deep teaching. *Encounter 16*(2), 25–7.

Wilson, R.A. (2003b). *Special Educational Needs in the Early Years*. London: Routledge.

Wilson, R.A. (2004). Why children play under the bushes. *Early Childhood News 16*(2), 14–21.

Wilson, R.A. (2010a). Goodness of fit: good for children and good for the Earth. In J.L. Hoot and J. Szente (eds), *The Earth is Our Home* (pp. 17–35). Washington, DC: Association for Childhood Education International.

Wilson, R.A. (2010b). The spiritual life of children. *Exchange 32*(5), 24–9.

Wilson, R.A. (2011). Becoming whole: developing an ecological identity. *Exchange 33*(3), 103–5.

Wilson, R.A., Kilmer, S.J. and Knauerhase, V. (1996). Developing an environmental outdoor play space. *Young Children 51*(6), 56–61.

Wright, J.L. and Shade, D.D. (1994). *Young Children: Active Learners in a Technological Age*. Washington, DC: NAEYC.

Zimowsky, P. (2008). Fight "nature deficit disorder": get kids outside. *The Olympian*, 13 December.

# Index